CREEPY CRYPTIDS

AND STRANGE UFO ENCOUNTERS OF PENNSYLVANIA
BIGFOOT, THUNDERBIRDS,
MYSTERIES OF THE CHESTNUT RIDGE AND MORE
CASEBOOK FOUR

© 2022 Stan Gordon. All rights reserved. This book or any portions or illustrations herein, may not be reproduced by any method or in any form without permission from the author.

The author has attempted to provide proper credit for any copyrighted material used in this book. If there are any corrections needed, please notify the author.

Interested parties may contact Stan Gordon at

PO. Box 936, Greensburg, PA 15601
via e-mail at paufo@comcast.net
or phone: 724-838-7768.

Up to date information on sightings and events can be found at
www.stangordon.info

ISBN 0966610857
First Edition

Printed in the United States of America

Cover and layout by Bulldog Design
bulldog.design.pa@gmail.com

Designed in Serif Affinity Publisher
Cover designed in FlowScape and Affinity Photo
Alien Miner figure by jibajadesign through CGTrader.com
Howlin' Mad font by Daniel Zadorozny of Iconian Fonts (www.iconian.com).

OTHER BOOKS BY STAN GORDON

Really Mysterious Pennsylvania
UFOs, Bigfoot & Other Weird Encounters Casebook One
ISBN-10: 0966610822

Silent Invasion
The Pennsylvania UFO-Bigfoot Casebook (Casebook Two)
ISBN-10: 0966610830

Astonishing Encounters
Pennsylvania's Unknown Creatures, Casebook Three
ISBN-10: 0966610849

Table of Contents

Dedication	5
Acknowledgments	7
Introduction	9
Chapter One Unidentified Flying Objects	15
Chapter Two Close Encounters with Mini-UFOs	67
Chapter Three Bigfoot Encounters	87
Chapter Four Thunderbird Sightings	117
Chapter Five What Mysterious Beasts Lurk Below the Water?	125
Chapter Six Those Mysterious Black Panthers	131
Chapter Seven Even Stranger Cryptid Incidents	145
Chapter Eight The Mysterious Chestnut Ridge and the Laurel Highlands of Pennsylvania	175
Chapter Nine Other Unusual Occurrences	185
Chapter Ten Bigfoot and Cryptid Mysterious Findings	187
Conclusion	199
About the Author	203
Contact Information	207
Index	209

Stan Gordon

DEDICATION

This book is dedicated to my three young grandsons, Peyton, Elijah, and Declan. They are three smart young boys who like to visit PapPap and look at his UFO and Bigfoot pictures. Peyton likes sports and video games. Elijah likes monsters and Godzilla, and Declan is just discovering the world around us and likes Bigfoot, too. Maybe someday one or more of the boys will help PapPap track down some of these mysterious reports.

My wife Debbie has been my inspiration to carry on my research, and her love and support keeps me going regardless of the obstacles that you sometimes encounter on this strange journey.

CREEPY CRYPTIDS

Stan Gordon

Acknowledgments

The public could never know the truth about these very strange ongoing reports without the witnesses who have shared their personal experiences with me. Many of these people had firsthand encounters that they could not explain and were reluctant to publicly talk about what took place.

Quite often they were glad to find out that other people have shared similar encounters and that they were not alone. Thanks to the witnesses who have shared their experiences so that others could learn that this is indeed a very strange world.

Historically, Fayette County in Southwest Pennsylvania is one of the most active areas in the state for ongoing mysterious encounters. This is especially true of locations that border or take place on the Chestnut Ridge.

For many years Jim Brown, a friend and an independent researcher with extensive technical experience, has been investigating UFOs, cryptids and other phenomena in that area. Jim and I have corresponded for many years on these incidents. In this book I have included a number of Jim's investigation reports on some of the strange cases that he examined. Thanks to Jim for permission to use these reports. You can find more about Jim's research by visiting his website at: www.jimsdestinations.com.

CREEPY CRYPTIDS

As I am writing this book, I was sad to learn that my friend, research associate and forensic bigfoot artist Dave Dragosin, had passed away. Dave had provided to me sketches of Bigfoot that were based on his interviews with eyewitnesses. He was a great guy and I will miss our conversations. Dave will surely be missed by those in the Bigfoot field, and he will always be remembered.

I would also like to thank the artists who have provided their sketches to be used in my books, such as Keith Bastianini, Charles Hanna, Robert McCurry, Rick Rieger, and Mike Soohey.

Thanks also to fellow researchers, Dwayne Pintoff, Eric Altman, and Kevin Paul for their input and sharing their experiences.

I want to give a special mention to my longtime friend, Tom Ankney, who is also a UFO witness. Tom saw a UFO in the 1960s over the Chestnut Ridge near Derry, PA. He went public for the first time when he was interviewed for the Small Town Monsters documentary, "Invasion On Chestnut Ridge".

Stan Gordon

INTRODUCTION

I was a ten-year-old inquisitive young fellow that had an interest in science and electronics. It was after hearing a talk radio show in 1959 discussing flying saucers, ghosts, and strange creatures, that my curiosity was stimulated to try to learn more about those subjects. I have been conducting in the field investigations of various phenomena since 1965, after the Kecksburg UFO incident took place about twelve miles from my hometown of Greensburg, Pennsylvania.

It became apparent when I started my investigations that most reports of an encounter with a UFO, Bigfoot, or other odd occurrences were reported by credible observers. I also soon realized, however, that many of these incidents, with proper investigation, could be explained as originating from a natural or man-made source.

In the years to follow, more and more detailed UFO observations and encounters with Bigfoot and other cryptids (creatures that have never been scientifically proven to exist) as well as other unusual incidents that took place could not be easily dismissed.

These mysterious occurrences were reported from men, women, and children of various age groups and backgrounds. Among the witnesses I interviewed over the years were scientists, engineers, schoolteachers, state troopers and municipal police officers, other first responders, former military personnel, commercial, private, and corporate pilots, air traffic controllers, experienced hunters and outdoorsmen, and many other professionals and trained observers.

Most of these witnesses were reluctant to even report what they had encountered and almost none wanted to be identified. They had nothing to gain by reporting their strange experiences. They were just looking for answers and wanted to know if anyone else had reported something similar.

Witnesses could report these experiences without any ridicule and could have remained anonymous if they so chose. I also do not give out exact locations where these encounters have taken place. These incidents often occurred on private property.

When I first began on site field investigations of UFO cases in 1965, there were many individuals in the UFO research field that felt that it was quite possible that some of the UFO encounters reported could be visitors from another planet. In the years to follow, I investigated multitudes of UFO incidents reported across Pennsylvania. It is now more apparent that there is likely more than one origin to the unexplained category of the UFO mystery.

There were lots of reports of high-altitude sightings of luminous objects zigzagging and maneuvering unlike conventional aircraft. There were also numerous significant UFO cases where what appeared to be large solid physical objects were observed at very close range and sometimes very low to the ground. Some witnesses said what they saw were disc, oval, cigar, triangular, and even rectangular in shape.

Witnesses reported that in some cases these objects appeared to be metallic and solid in appearance and were apparently constructed devices. During the 1960s, in Pennsylvania, residents claimed that they not only observed what appeared to be portholes or windows on some of these objects, but at times they also observed humanoid occupants as well.

During the 1960s, I also became aware that there were other UFO encounters being reported that were quite different from the more common UFO descriptions. I have called these encounters with "mini-UFOs" since these objects are generally of a reduced size. I have investigated numerous such reports in the years since I first heard of such cases.

These encounters continue to be reported and they are often seen very close to the observers. There will be more details about this in a separate chapter in this book.

You might find it of interest that during my nearly lifetime of investigating these strange reports, I have never personally seen a UFO or Bigfoot. I have no doubt, however, that many credible eyewitnesses have seen mysterious creatures, unknown aerial objects, and have experienced various other phenomena that is not easily dismissed.

The Early 1970s

It was soon after I established a hotline to report UFO sightings in 1969 that it became apparent that I would be unable to handle the large volume of strange incident reports that were being phoned in.

In 1970, I established a volunteer research group to investigate UFO sightings as well as other phenomena. That was the Westmoreland County UFO Study Group (WCUFOSG). It was the first of three such groups that I would organize that would investigate mysterious incidents across Pennsylvania for many years.

The WCUFOSG initially began in Westmoreland County, extended its research coverage into the Pittsburgh area, and by

CREEPY CRYPTIDS

1973 was investigating mysterious incidents across Pennsylvania. The group became well known and would often have UFO reports or other strange cases referred by law enforcement or by the news media.

The group had many research specialists who volunteered their time and experience to conduct field investigations into these reports. Among the group were scientists, engineers, technicians, former military specialists, and police officers.

Many of the members remained anonymous because of their positions at that time. Some of these individuals worked for major research companies in the Pittsburgh area such as Westinghouse, Gulf and Alcoa. Some of those people who got involved in these investigations were initially quite skeptical of UFO sightings and Bigfoot or other similar subjects. Some of those people spent years with me conducting on-scene investigations.

With my electronics background, I set up a high-tech radio communications center in my home that served as the groups' operations center. A two-way radio dispatch system was activated so that we could keep in touch with some of the field investigators and could direct them to a sighting location.

As the years passed by, many of these researchers who were initially skeptical had the opportunity to interview witnesses and to see the emotional responses of some of those people. They examined physical evidence at the scene, and they noticed the similarity of the details among the cases being reported. Many of those researchers, in time, began to realize that there were indeed some very strange cases that could not be easily explained. The question was then and still remains today- just what are we dealing with?

Stan Gordon

It was during the early 1970s that some rather strange incidents came to my attention that began to make me wonder as to just what was taking place. During 1972, a series of incidents took place along a wooded area bordering Humphrey Road outside of Greensburg, just miles from where I lived.

Residents who had lived there for years were suddenly reporting strange screams and howls from the woods, large, unusual footprints, and sightings of a creature similar to other Bigfoot reports. They were also hearing the sound of something large and bipedal walking in the woods. Locals were also reporting strange lights low to the ground and near their homes.

Then a major series of UFO sightings began at the start of 1973 and continued all year. Numerous close range UFO encounters took place across the state and many cases were reported in the news. It was during the summer of that year that things became even more fascinating when numerous Bigfoot sightings were reported by the public.

The strangeness of these incidents began to increase when cases were reported that UFOs and Bigfoot had been seen together at the same time and place. One incident involved multiple witnesses where a large UFO landed on a field and two Bigfoot in the same field at the same time. In another case, a Bigfoot was observed carrying a small luminous sphere of light. Then even stranger, a woman shot at a Bigfoot only six feet away with her 16-gauge shot gun. The creature suddenly vanished in a bright flash of light. Minutes later, a UFO appeared over the nearby trees.

These cases are described in detail in my book, "Silent Invasion: The Pennsylvania UFO-Bigfoot Casebook". It was during that time period that I began to hear recurring statements from various witnesses suggesting that Bigfoot is even stranger than I had ever imagined.

These cases have continued to occur over the years, not only in Pennsylvania, but also from throughout the country and elsewhere. It has become more apparent that Bigfoot and some other cryptids could be much more unusual than just unknown animals. You will read many accounts in this book that suggest that possibility.

Stan Gordon

Chapter One

Unidentified Flying Objects

What is this Mystery Object?
June 16, 1980

On June 16, 1980, an unusual incident occurred in a rural location not far from Herminie in Westmoreland County, Pennsylvania. It was about 9:30 PM, when the lady of the house was in her bedroom and noticed a bright object about the size of a car headlight hovering near some trees behind the house. She opened the window but heard no noise. Several minutes later when she returned to the window, the bright light was gone.

The next day, her husband discovered a strange metallic object sticking out of the ground on the hill behind the house. The object, which weighed a little over twenty pounds, was over twenty one inches long, and looked like two metallic cones that had been welded together. My PASU research group investigated the case many years ago.

A laboratory analysis indicated that the object was determined to be one hundred percent stainless steel. The object appeared to be hollow. There have been theories over the years as to what the object was, but nothing conclusive so far. The family involved was very credible and were perplexed over the incident.

UFO Lifts Car on Blair County Roadway October 15, 1983

A very strange encounter took place on the evening of October 15, 1983, in Blair County. The witness, Catherine Burk, was traveling north on Route 220 near the community of Bellwood. The time was about 8:30 PM when the witness had a very strange experience.

The evening was dark and overcast as the woman drove her 1976 Chevy Malibu at about 35 mph. It was near the turnoff to the town Bellwood when an unusual whirling sound was heard from the right side of the road. That is when she noticed a brilliant disc that was completely silver in color that had a protruding rounded area underneath. There were no windows or flashing lights observed. She estimated that the object was about twenty four feet in diameter.

The object was very low and only about thirty feet above the ground. As the strange object passed overhead, the right side of the car suddenly lifted up about two to three feet off the road. The driver put her weight toward the other seat attempting to level the vehicle. However, she kept ending up in her driving area.

While off the ground, Mrs. Burk realized that the car functions were not properly working. She tried turning the steering wheel but was unable to do so, and the headlights were only working intermittently.

The car was off the ground for several seconds before it leveled out. She felt the vehicle hit the ground hard. She was then knocked against the dash of the car hitting her shoulder area. As soon as the car struck the road surface, the motor stalled. Mrs. Burk was able to move the car off the road. The object continued moving off across the sky as it departed from the area. It took over twenty minutes before she was able to start the engine.

When she finally arrived home, she talked with her daughter about what had taken place and the Bellwood police were contacted. The Bellwood police chief Gregory Ciaccio, was interviewed by Marsha Heim, a reporter for the local Altoona Mirror newspaper. The newspaper also interviewed Mrs. Burk about her strange experience. In the interviews that I conducted with Mrs. Burk, she seemed very credible and respectable. She had no real interest in the UFO subject and didn't believe in aliens.

Soon after the incident, the witness began to experience a number of physical effects that she believed were associated with her UFO encounter. Among the effects reported were some hearing losses in her right ear, severe headaches, and pain in her shoulder and neck area. She also mentioned that she had been having trouble sleeping after the encounter.

There was another strange element to this already mysterious event. It was a neighbor that brought this activity to the attention of Mrs. Burk. It was early one morning a few days after the encounter that a man in a suit driving a dark navy-blue car arrived where her car was parked. The man had in his hands what appeared to be a tray with long strips of tape on it.

He proceeded to apply the tape strips and attach them over various sections of her automobile, as if trying to pick up any residue. Then in November, two more mystery men in dark suits showed up again and they also had trays of tape. She watched as they spent nearly forty five minutes applying and retrieving the tape from all over the vehicle body. It appeared that someone else had an interest in this close-range UFO encounter as well.

Mrs. Burk and I had numerous telephone discussions and mail correspondence after the encounter took place. She was a very nice woman, and I was convinced that Mrs. Burk was an honest and truthful individual, and that she did experience something very strange that day in 1983.

Addendum: There were other UFO researchers who conducted investigations concerning this incident such as T. Scott Crain Jr., Larry G. McKee, Lynn Sanderson and others. Their research helped document the details of what occurred concerning this unusual UFO case.

Four Cornered Hovering Object Causes Physical Effects to Woman and her Dog
November 21, 1993

On the evening of November 21, 1993, I received a phone call from a woman who sounded very frightened and told me of the UFO encounter that she and her dog had experienced just a short time ago that same evening. I packed up my gear and headed to her location a few miles outside of Greensburg. I noticed that it was a very clear sky and cool night. I later checked the weather data. The temperature was 30 degrees and visibility was ten miles.

Stan Gordon

I arrived a short time later. The woman was visibly shaken, and she was holding her dog as she told me how they had been affected by the object that hovered low above them. I learned the following during my interview with the witness.

The woman was taking her dog outside at about 10:45 PM. She noticed that it was unusually quiet at the time and no cars were driving through the area. Her dog was walking around in the yard while the lady was cleaning up in the kennel area. Moments later she realized that she wasn't hearing the sound of the bell on the dog's collar.

She looked around the yard and found the dog standing completely still. The dog was looking skyward with glazed eyes. She looked up and was amazed to see a large solid object moving very slowly about sixty feet just above a telephone pole.

Her first thought was that it was some type of unusual aircraft that was about to crash, but soon realized that this was something much more unusual. She described seeing a very large and solid triangular object with an extra point. The object that appeared larger than her house had a smooth surface and was a medium gun gray metal color.

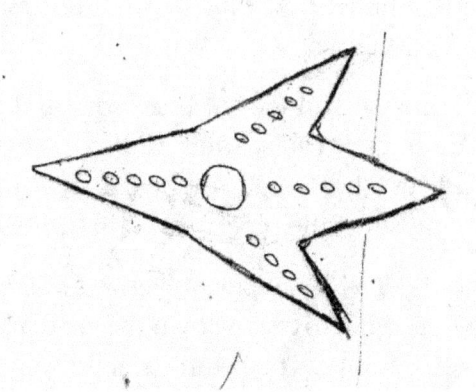

Drawing of the object used with permission of the witness.

CREEPY CRYPTIDS

There were at least two to three white round lights on each of the points of the object. The lights became whiter and brighter as more were turned on. The witness commented that those lights were made up of the purest white light she had ever seen. At the bottom center of the object was what was described as a huge dark red light that seemed intimidating to the witness. The red light was much larger than the white lights.

The witness also could hear a humming sound emitting from the strange hovering device. Moments later, the object was hovering overhead. It was then that more lights came on each point and beams of white light shined down from the object directly onto the woman and the dog. During the time they were illuminated, the dog didn't move, remained quiet and was focused on the object hovering overhead.

The woman seemed to be confused with her thinking while in the beams of light. The woman said she was extremely frightened during the sighting. She said that she experienced a severe pain in the center of her forehead.

She put the dog down to go inside the kennel, but the dog refused to follow her orders and instead cowered at the right side of the shelter. The lady commented that it was the first time the dog didn't obey her commands.

She ran into the house and locked the doors and called a friend who had a police and fire call scanner radio to see if he had heard about an airplane crash. He had not heard anything, and he told her to look out and see if the object was still in the area.

She went back outside and saw the object was still there above the kennel. The object began to move down the road and over the roof of some neighbor's homes. The beams of light were gone, and she could only see the white lights on the corners of the object. The witness ran to the back of her home to try to get a better look.

Stan Gordon

It was then that she noticed an odd white and gray cloud formation that appeared to have its own luminosity. At that time, she heard a humming sound and a high frequency pitch in the area.

Her friend arrived about ten minutes later and he also heard the strange sounds and saw the odd clouds as well. By the time I arrived, all of the activity had ceased. The lady commented that after she and the dog went inside after the incident, the dog seemed agitated, and wouldn't sit or lay down, and just continued to walk around.

This witness was very credible and was quite upset over the experience. Within twenty four hours, there were two additional UFO reports within several miles of each other.

Addendum

It was about ten minutes prior to this sighting, that another UFO sighting took place only miles away off Donahue Road. An object also reported to be the size of a house with beams of light emitting from it and only about one hundred feet above the ground had been observed. The witness also heard a humming sound as the object passed low overhead.

The next evening, November 22, 1993, a group of people in Mount Pleasant Township watched an object rise up out of a field. The object looked boomerang shaped with a few lights on it. There was a white light on each corner of the object and a red light in the bottom center. The object was estimated to be about sixty feet long. The silent object moved off across the sky then made a turn and went out of sight.

CREEPY CRYPTIDS

Stealth-Like Object Passes Over Route 30 Near Greensburg, Westmoreland County
October 31, 2009

It was about 7 PM on October 31, 2009, when a man traveling down Route 30 East outside of Greensburg and something unusual caught his attention as he approached the red light near Home Depot. Out of the corner of his eye, he observed a large bright white light moving across the sky towards the highway. His first thought was that it was a bright meteor or a navigational light on an airplane.

As the traffic signal changed green and the light passed over the roadway, the driver slowed down and hung his head out the window and was amazed at what he was seeing. The car ahead of him in the other lane had also slowed down as well.

The moving light appeared to have slowed in speed. The driver was then able to discern a somewhat triangular shape which was surrounded in light. Having been in the military and familiar with aircraft, he described it as being shaped, "like a fighter jet with its tail end down and nose up".

The object was dark in color, possibly black or gray. It was quite large and solid in structure. The object passed over the highway at about one thousand feet altitude and it was completely silent. A bright white light surrounded the solid dark object. There also seemed to be a cloudy mass around the dark shape as well.

The object continued to move across the sky towards the direction of Hempfield High School. The witness said that before he lost sight of it, the object turned and traveled at an angle, but soon was lost from sight in the trees. He drove to the Giant Eagle parking lot where he had a good view of the area, but the object was not seen again. The witness stated that he still gets chills when talking about what he saw.

Stan Gordon

The Case of the Noisy Cylindrical Shaped Object December 23, 2009

A man was inside of his home and doing some computer work on the evening of December 23, 2009, when he heard a rumbling sound coming from outside. The sound was similar to fireworks going off in the distance.

He went outside to see what was creating the sound and looked skyward. The witness observed a very large cylindrical shaped object which was estimated to be about three hundred feet long. There was a bright white light positioned both at the front and back of the object and no sound was heard while it was observed moving very slowly in the sky. The object appeared to be about one thousand to fifteen hundred feet in altitude and seemed to be north of Kittanning and moving towards Freeport.

The startled man ran inside of his home to find a camera so he could take a picture of the cylindrical shaped object. He returned moments later but the object was gone. To the fellow's surprise, in just about the same position in the sky was a huge triangular shaped pattern of lights, which seemed to be about the size of the former object.

The shape of the triangle was comprised of four non-blinking white lights with a soft red pulsating light in the center of the object. The pattern of the lights and the movement suggested that they were attached to a larger construction.

This object, which was also moving very slowly and was silent, was observed for about thirty seconds as trees blocked the view of the object as it moved across the sky. The man did try to take a picture with his camera, but he was unable to because he could not find the object in the small viewfinder. The witness told me that he would never forget what he had seen.

CREEPY CRYPTIDS

Luminous Object Photographed in Hempfield Township July 18, 2010

It was just about 9:30 PM when several independent witnesses observed a bright object moving slowly and steadily across the sky. One man and his wife were sitting in their backyard when a neighbor yelled to him and asked him what was in the sky. They all observed a bright orange-yellow glowing object moving slowly below the clouds.

Another couple walking down the road spotted the object at the same time. One witness told me that it looked like a big ball that moved steadily and made no sound. Another spotter got his binoculars and said that the object had an orange flickering to it, but it wasn't on fire.

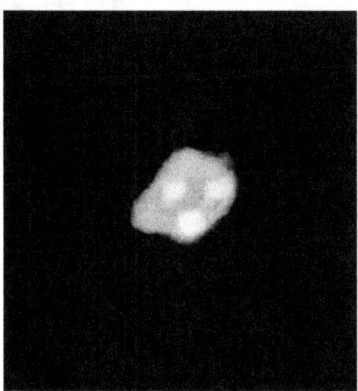

Photo used with permission of the witness.

One witness obtained his iPhone and used the camera setting to take several pictures and video footage of the object. The object seemed to accelerate in speed as it moved out of sight. Upon examination, at least one picture clearly shows a series of three white lights in a triangular pattern.

Stan Gordon

Daylight Cigar Shaped UFO Hovers Low Over Field
August 22, 2011

At about 9 AM, a man was traveling on Rt. 228 at about 45 mph when he observed something off to his left. About a quarter of a mile away, he noticed a large object hovering over a field. What he saw looked like a big cigar or "like an airplane with no wings".

The object appeared to hover over a field about two hundred to two hundred fifty feet off the ground. The sun was glaring off the side of the object. The fuselage shape appeared to be stainless steel or chrome and was very shiny. In the center of the object there appeared to be a darker area which was estimated to be about ten percent of the length.

The witness estimated that it was one hundred eighty to two hundred feet in length from that distance. There were no lights visible. The witness had pulled off the road to the left into a parking lot where five to seven other cars had pulled over to look at the object. The man said he was very excited and called his wife after watching it for about four minutes. He then realized that he might have a camera and started looking for it. He was about to take a picture when the object suddenly just "vanished" and was not seen again.

Huge Round Object Hovers Near Highway
November 24, 2012

It was during the early morning hours of November 24, 2012, when a motorist observed something strange in the sky near Waynesburg. It was unlike anything he had ever seen. It was about 12:30 AM, when the man driving on Route 79 South traveling towards Waynesburg observed a large object in the sky along the highway.

CREEPY CRYPTIDS

The silent object was hovering about two hundred feet or less above a group of trees, which were about six hundred feet away. The witness at first thought that it might have been a blimp, but the shape, which was easily seen from the light given off from the object, appeared dark or black and had no fins. The object, according to the witness, "was huge" and about one hundred to one hundred twenty five feet long. It was estimated to be seventy five to eighty feet in height.

The rounded object was covered with many lights. The middle section of the object contained numerous round white lights that were steady in intensity. There were numerous smaller white lights that covered the rest of the object. On the top right side of the craft, there were white lights observed that were flashing slowly.

The witness slowed down and observed the object for about a minute or more. This is one aspect of the observation that really shook up the man. As he explained to me, he had been watching the object, then seconds later he looked back as he passed it and it was nowhere in sight. "It was just gone." The man stated to me, "that really freaked me out."

Fast Moving Object Splits from Formation of Lights
February 9, 2013

The witness in North Huntingdon had just walked outside on to his porch to get some fresh air that evening. He happened to look up into the clear sky towards the north when he observed about four to six lights that appeared in a somewhat check-mark like formation. The lights appeared round and bright orange in color. When the witness first saw them, his first thought was that these were military aircraft. As the man continued to watch, it was soon realized that the lights appeared to be stationary and made no sound.

Stan Gordon

Seconds later, about three to four of the objects suddenly disappeared. In a few moments, the witness watched as one of the remaining orange lights, which seemed to have been positioned at the furthest section of the formation, suddenly shot off at a very fast rate of speed towards the north. The witness said that it might have had a slight trail behind it as it moved off and that it looked similar to a meteor but didn't break up as they usually do.

The witness quickly called a neighbor to come outside and take a look. That neighbor was able to view the last light along with the primary witness. That light moved very slowly towards the southeast, and they watched as it moved far off in the distance but had changed to a white color and looked similar to a satellite moving across the sky. The total observation time by the primary witness was about a minute.

UFO Formation "Like a Train in the Sky" Over Greensburg
March 9, 2013

A man was outside doing some stargazing on the evening of March 9, 2013, when he observed something that startled him and has left him baffled. The witness was looking up into the clear dark sky when at about 9:30 PM, he observed seven to nine objects toward the southeast. The man was startled by what he was seeing, and he told me that the best way to describe it was that they looked "like a train in the sky".

When I went to the location of the sighting to interview the witness, he pointed out the path that the objects took as they moved high over downtown Greensburg. The objects each appeared to be rectangular in shape and seemed similar to boxcars.

Each one looked identical in that they appeared yellowish gold in color, and the surface appeared to be speckled with a slight gold illumination. All of the objects looked as though they had a texture of lighted bumps. The witness explained to me that these didn't appear to be separated lights but a constant illumination.

They all moved together in formation like ducks, however, they were not in a V, rather in a staggered diagonal line. The witness could see the sky between each object, and there was nothing connected to them. As the silent objects continued to move, they all kept about the same distance from each other.

Sketch of objects in formation. Used with permission of the witness

The objects never changed positions and remained perfectly in formation as they traveled. The objects moved high above and to the right of the county courthouse and continued to move smoothly towards the northwest.

The objects were observed for about ten to twelve seconds before the view of the objects was blocked by trees and houses. The formation was silent and moved consistently in the same formation and never changed speed or direction. The witness estimated that from their distance and altitude, the objects appeared to be quite large.

Addendum: I received other independent reports on this same night and around the same time frame from other observers who watched something unusual in the sky.

Possible Military Jet UFO Pursuit
April 17, 2013

On the evening of April 17, 2013, I received a phone call from the father of a young man who, along with several other fellows, had observed something strange in the sky that evening. The father had called me at 8:17 PM, and the incident had reportedly occurred about fifteen minutes previous to the call. At that time, I talked with both the father and the witness concerning what had taken place.

The father told me that he was picking up his son at his place of employment outside of Latrobe. When he got to the location, he noticed his son and some other employees looking up at the sky. He didn't know what was going on and didn't get out of the car to find out. When his son got in the car, he told his father about a strange event that had occurred in the distant sky. After talking with his son about the incident, the man contacted me.

I learned from his son that he had just finished his work shift and was exiting through the rear entrance of the building when he noticed several coworkers looking up at the sky. There was still some light out, and it was off in the distance towards the west that he observed a strange object at a very high altitude.

The witness at first thought that it was the fuselage of a helicopter. The object appeared to be dropping straight down from the sky "like a bomb falling". The object was black in color, and long and narrow in shape. There were what appeared to be about four large round lights on the side.

The object was dropping and spinning as it fell. Suddenly, he noticed what appeared to be two military jets with contrails approaching in the sky. The first jet came from the east and began to close in on the object approaching it from the back.

The second aircraft approached from the west and came straight toward the object. The witness told me at that time that there appeared to have been some interaction between the aircraft and the black object. The fellow is unsure what occurred, but he believes the aircraft either bumped or fired on the object, at which time the object suddenly began to spin and descend faster.

The object continued to fall lower in the sky but was lost from sight by the observers. The two aircraft then departed from the area, moving back toward the direction they originated from.

The entire observation lasted about three minutes. As of this writing, I still have been unable to talk with the other observers. I hope to be able to do this at some future time.

I did learn that a resident of Latrobe was walking his dog at about 8 PM, when he noticed an odd aircraft contrail towards the western sky. The man said this contrail stood out because it was shorter and brighter than others he normally has seen.

Silent Rectangular Object Hovers Low Over Route 30 in North Huntingdon
June 1, 2013

At approximately 10:05 PM, the witness and her three-year-old child had just pulled out of the Sheetz convenience store on Route

30 in North Huntingdon Township. At the red light, the driver made a left on U.S. Route 30 and proceeded East toward Greensburg. The woman had a window down and the car radio was playing at the time. As she moved along the highway just a short distance, away her attention was drawn to a large object hovering over Route 30.

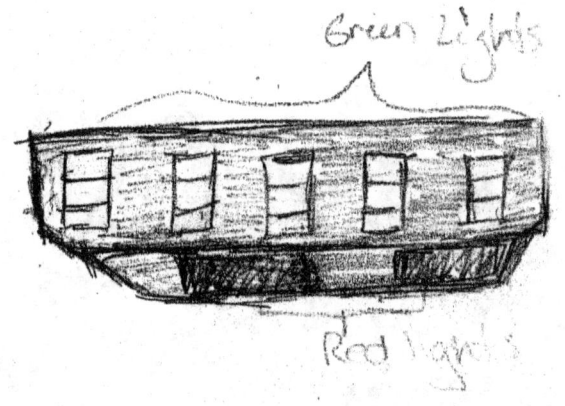

Sketch used with permission of the witness

As she slowed down and approached closer, she recalled saying out loud, "What in the world is that?" Her young child who was in the backseat responded by saying, "Look Mommy, a flying I-pad in the sky". The woman looked around and noticed that there were no other cars at the time on that stretch of the road. She was quite concerned over what the object was, and initially stopped on the highway, about one hundred fifty feet away from the hovering object. She was trying to figure out in her mind a logical explanation for what she was seeing.

The object, which was completely silent, was hovering approximately sixty feet above that section of the roadway. The witness described the object as looking, "mostly rectangular," and told me that it "looked like the gondola of a blimp without the blimp." The length of the solid object appeared to extend over the east and westbound lanes of the highway. The object was estimated to be about fifty five feet in length, and approximately thirty five to forty feet tall.

Stretch of Route 30 where UFO incident took place

The witness described the object as being two tiered. The top section was made up of five sets of green lights. There were three individual rectangular lights in each set. The five sets of lights were all evenly spaced in a vertical position, and the lights were all steady with no blinking.

The witness said the green color was brighter than the green of a traffic light. The bottom section, which was smaller in size, contained within it two long solid red lights that were placed side by side. The two lights were steady and never blinked. They gave the witness the impression of looking like brake lights, but they were huge.

The woman quickly called her mother using the blue tooth cell phone hookup in her car. She asked her mother if she knew of any explanation for the object that was hovering ahead of her over the road. As the car passed underneath the object, the woman noticed that the digital display on her car dashboard for the clock, temperature, air bag status, radio, and Bluetooth sync suddenly blacked out.

The FM radio station she was listening to lost signal. She also lost her cell phone signal. The witness attempted to take a picture of the object with her iPhone, but the camera function wouldn't load up.

She accelerated down the road to get away from the object. About a half mile away she looked back towards where the object had been and could no longer see it. The digital displays all returned to normal, her radio came back on and she was able to make cell phone contact again with her mother as she approached the Adamsburg exit. When she got home and discussed what happened with her family, they asked her to draw a sketch of the object while it was still clear in her memory.

I conducted both telephone and face to face interviews with the witness and her family and I also went to the location of the incident. The witness works out of the area but travels that road daily to go back and forth to work. A part of the investigation included examining the vehicle driven that day. Due to the woman's work schedule, it was several days after the incident before the car could be tested. No magnetic anomalies or abnormal radiation levels were found.

The witness said that she drove down that same section of road several days after the incident trying to make sense of what she saw. She was looking for a tower or even a balloon from a car dealership to explain what she saw but could find nothing to explain the object. She also was upset that her young child continues to look skyward for the "floating I-pad".

The witness tells me that this was an experience she will never forget. She told me how she is the kind of person who must have an explanation for nearly everything in life and now there remains the question of, "What did I see?"

Addendum: One of the first UFO cases I investigated occurred in August of 1966, just down the road from where this encounter took place. That incident occurred at the Adamsburg exit and involved an object hovering over the 500-kilovolt high tension power line. As two people in a car on Route 30 approached the power line, the object dropped below the power line and came at the car so close that the occupants ducked their heads. That case is mentioned in my first book, "Really Mysterious Pennsylvania".

Daylight Sighting of Elongated Object Near Madison, PA January 29, 2014

On the afternoon of January 29, 2014, two people were traveling in a car on a country road about one mile outside the borough of Madison when they noticed something very unusual in the sky. A strange object could be seen as they continued their journey, but the view of the object was obstructed by trees along the road. The driver pulled over at a clearing to get a better look at the object that appeared to be motionless. The object was estimated to be about a mile up in the sunny sky.

The craft according to one witness looked to be cigar shaped. He stated to me during an interview, "it looked like a cruise missile but sitting still." The other observer thought the object looked more rectangular and quite long. The object was either white or silver in color, as that was unclear due to the sun reflecting off the surface of the object.

The silent object had no windows, propellers, or markings. The two observers were able to see the left side of the craft from their position. They did notice what appeared to be a small wing which was very stubby along the left side. They did not notice any other wing structures.

They watched the object for about thirty seconds while it hovered. The object suddenly moved off and traveled toward Pittsburgh. As the object moved across the sky, no propeller or engine sound were heard.

The witnesses had never seen anything like this before. One thought was that this was some type of new drone operating in the area and coinciding with the Presidential visit that same afternoon in Pittsburgh. The description is unlike any of the drone prototypes that I am familiar with.

Black Cigar Shaped Object Rises From Cloud, Indiana County September 3, 2014

Photo used with permission of the witness.

The witness was hiking on the afternoon of September 3, 2014, in a rural location of Indiana County, not far from the Homer City Power Station. The weather was partly cloudy and about eighty degrees. About 2 PM he noticed some movement in the sky. He observed a cigar shaped object that was moving in and out of a cloud. The object was black and appeared to be hazy and not sharply outlined.

The object was a distance away and continued to watch as the cigar shaped object continued going in and out of the cloud. The man grabbed his camera and took several pictures. As the man watched this activity, the object was suddenly lost from sight. He was unsure where the object had gone to. Total observation was about a minute.

Huge Cigar Shaped Object Hovers Over Chestnut Ridge September 24, 2014

Researcher Jim Brown has been investigating a UFO sighting that occurred on September 24, 2014, outside of Fairchance in Fayette County.

It was around 7 PM when the witness observed what was described as a single huge cigar shaped object that appeared low on the eastern horizon over the Chestnut Ridge.

The object was described as hazy and gold-orange in color. The object appeared to hover over the ridge area and never moved or changed appearance during the nearly ten minutes that it was being observed.

Then while under observation, the object suddenly vanished from sight and was not observed again. It never moved away from its position or showed any motion or deformity.

Note: The hazy description of the cigar shaped object is similar to what was described by a witness on September 3, 2014, in Indiana County. The Chestnut Ridge area along Westmoreland, Fayette, and Indiana counties continues to be active yearly with reports of UFOs, and other strange encounters.

Stan Gordon

Glowing Football Observed in the Sky in Butler County
February 6, 2015

It was late afternoon on February 6, 2015, when a man relaxing on his back porch located in a rural area not far from Cranberry, observed something unusual in the sky. He noticed a very large luminous object moving steadily from the south to the northeast.

The man thought at first that it was a satellite, but then realized that the object was much too large and was much lower in altitude than a satellite would travel. The man yelled for his wife who came out and she observed the object as well. The object was described as an oval shaped object that looked like, "a glowing football". The object was glowing white, made no sound, and no lights were observed on it.

The object moved at a steady fast speed but not like that of a meteor. As the two observers continued to watch the object as it moved off in the distance it suddenly "blinked out" and vanished. The observation lasted about two minutes.

Object Engulfs Car in Light
April 17, 2015

The following incident occurred Westmoreland County, Pennsylvania at a rural location not far from West Newton. The incident is believed to have occurred on April 17, 2015. It was between 10:30 and 11 PM that evening, when two people heard some engine noises down the road from where they lived. They got into their vehicle and proceeded down the road to see if someone was trespassing on their property.

They pulled off the country road and shut off their car to listen for any voices or engine sounds. They were sitting there for a short time when they both noticed a bright white light in the distance that was moving in their direction. As they continued to watch, the light began to make a circular pattern in the sky. The object then approached closer to their location and hovered over some trees.

What they saw was a large solid round white light that didn't blink. They at first thought it might be a helicopter, but this object became stationary and made no sound. The fellow in the vehicle wanted to get out and walk closer to the object to get a better look at it but was advised not to leave the car.

As they sat there staring at the light, they suddenly became surrounded in a dim white light emitting from the object. The witnesses were hesitant to call it a beam, but it lit up the car and the immediate area. One witness said it was similar to the light you might see in a dimly lit living room area.

The two people in the car heard no sound and did not experience any odd effects while they were engulfed in the light. Soon after the light came on, the driver started the car and quickly left the area. That person told me of having been frightened during the incident.

Huge Flying Box Observed Over the Allegheny River April 21, 2015

Two people traveling in their vehicle observed something very strange on the morning of April 21, 2015. The couple was traveling between Parker and East Brady around 10:30 or 11 AM, when they saw a flash of light in the sky. The viewing conditions were partly cloudy, with some dark thick clouds scattered about in many parts of the sky.

The flash was apparently the sun reflecting for a moment off the surface of a very large solid object. The couple pulled their car over to take a better look. The strange flying thing appeared to be in the distance over the Allegheny River.

The object was positioned near a large dark cloud and was described as similar to a "flying box". The rectangular object looked solid black and seemed to have four rows of windows or indentations on its surface. One witness said the object was huge and he estimated that it was seventy five hundred to ten thousand feet in altitude.

As the couple watched, the small building sized craft slowly moved inside a large dark cloud. The man in the car grabbed a camera and had it focused to take a picture of the object when it exited the cloud that it had entered. They waited forty five minutes, but the object was never seen again. They couldn't understand how something that large could have been lost from sight.

UFO Sightings Reported the Same Evening May 30, 2015

Witnesses near Monessen, PA, reported seeing a series of odd lights in the sky at about 10:45 PM on May 30, 2015. A total of six bright orange lights were observed moving from the direction of North Charleroi and moving towards Monessen and the area of the Monongahela River. The lights were seen moving one after the other and seemed to be about a half mile apart as they crossed the sky. The bright objects made no sound while being observed.

At about 11 PM, two observers outside of Mount Pleasant observed something unusually high in altitude in the night sky. They first saw a bright white light moving fast across the sky. From the object, they saw what was described as red-orange laser light beams that extending out across the sky. A short time later, the light beams went out. At the end sections of where the beams had been, they saw a white blinking light appear for a short time.

The blinking lights then began to shoot across the sky in various directions. The main white object moved toward a cloud and blinked out and was gone. Then moments later, a second bright white light approached from the opposite direction. It was at a much higher altitude than the first light. As the fellows watched, the same odd light activity began to take place as had occurred with the first object. Total observation time was about two minutes.

UFO Seen Falling From Sky From Johnstown Area August 28, 2015

At about 9:50 PM, a group of people were outside of a residence near Johnstown, PA, when one of them pointed to the sky and asked, "What is that?" The observers were familiar with the aircraft that are constantly seen landing and departing from the John Murtha Johnstown-Cambria County airport. What they saw was quite unusual. They could make out a series of lights that appeared attached to an object, but the shape was unclear.

What was observed appeared to be at the altitude of a small aircraft such as a Piper Cub ascending from the airport. It was moving towards the direction of Pittsburgh. They saw a bright red non-blinking light in the center that looked to be elongated. On each side of the red light was a non-blinking cream-colored light. As the lights passed overhead, they heard no sound.

Some of the witnesses ran out to the driveway to follow the path of the object. The object was steadily moving, and they watched it as it moved off in the distance toward the Laurel Ridge near Ligonier.

At that point, the object looked different, and they saw something that caused the observers concern. Over the mountains, the object "looked like a clear bubble with a fuzzy looking outside edge". Suddenly, that object dropped straight down from the sky towards the ground. Those watching expected there would be an impact and explosion. However, they heard and saw nothing after that.

Addendum: In recent years, other witnesses around this general area have also reported seeing an object high in the sky that suddenly drops straight down to the ground without any explosion or crashes being reported.

Boomerang Shaped Object Seen Near Springdale, PA September 1, 2015

The witness had just arrived home at around 10:30 PM, when she noticed a very bright white light in the sky towards the west. A loud sound was noticed as the light approached closer. The sound was unlike that of a medical helicopter or other propeller driven aircraft. It also didn't sound like a jet engine. The light appeared low in altitude. It was so bright and huge as it passed overhead that witness was able to determine it was not a medical helicopter.

The witness looked up and observed the bottom of a very large boomerang shaped object. There were what appeared to be evenly spaced dim white spotlights along the edge of the underside of the object. The lights each had a pale-yellow tinge and were non-blinking.

The underbelly of the object had a greenish tinge to it, something like the color of an avocado. The object continued to emit the loud noise as it moved toward the east, then banked towards the south and quickly moved out of sight. The witness estimated that the object was less than one thousand feet in altitude. The witness wonders what she saw that day.

Light and Smoke Trail Observed Over the Derry Ridge November 25, 2015

During the evening of November 25, 2015, over the Derry Side of the Chestnut Ridge, a witness was looking at the beautiful moon. Her attention was soon drawn to the right side of the moon where she noticed a bright white light followed by a smoke trail moving straight up into the sky. The witness commented, "It looked like a rocket".

The light and smoke trail appeared to suddenly stop. A short time later the light and smoke trail began to move again. The witness took her eyes off of that area for a moment but noticed a bright flash in the sky from that same area. When she looked back, the bright object had disappeared and only the smoke trail was still visible.

Luminous Object Separates in Sky
June 2016

June 11, 2016. In a rural area near Jeannette, several people observed a series of orange objects that looked similar to meteors. However, they had no tails and were slow moving. While under observation, one object broke apart and separated into two similar objects that moved across the sky in different directions.

A similar sighting occurred near Leechburg in Armstrong County on June 16th, where other witnesses reported up to ten luminous objects in the sky that were blinking orange then white in color. At one point, two of the objects joined together, then separated and moved off in different directions.

A Daylight Morphing UFO Near Uniontown
October 16, 2016

During the afternoon, a couple was driving down Route 43 in Fayette County outside of Uniontown. They were approaching the crest of a hill when a black misty smoke cloud appeared above some trees and began to form into a large black rectangular object. The object moved over the two left southbound lanes of the highway.

It then quickly moved over the northbound lanes that they were traveling on towards Pittsburgh. As the object nearly cleared those lanes, it suddenly stopped and formed a circular shape that was not as solid as the rectangular object had looked. It quickly re-formed back into the rectangular shape and moved back over the southbound lanes of the highway then suddenly just vanished from sight and was not seen again.

Object Falls From Sky Into the Monongahela River November 8, 2016

Screen shot capture. The picture is used with permission of the witness.

During the afternoon a man had just left work and was walking to his car in downtown Pittsburgh. He noticed high in the sky what appeared to be a cylinder-shaped object that looked as though it was hovering but had some movement to it. The object then seemed to drop from that altitude and smoke appeared to be emitting from the object.

As the object fell, it was blocked from view by the parkway. The man started videotaping as he ran in that direction. The object was blocked from view at its lowest level, but the witness saw it for a second over the Monongahela River. The object appeared to descend fast yet almost gliding.

The witness had the opinion that the object was metallic, and he noticed some type of triangle near the rear section. The witness believes the object fell into the river. The witness was able to capture some screen shots of the object from the video footage he had taken.

CREEPY CRYPTIDS

Misty Fog Surrounds Triangular Object
November 11, 2016

A man located in York County was outside talking on his phone that evening when he noticed an unusual object in the sky that appeared to be gliding. The object was three dimensional and looked like a very large metallic triangular object.

The object was dark gray in color and appeared to have a white foggy mist surrounding it. The witness could clearly see the side of the craft that was visible to him. He also had a very good view of the underside of the object. There were a number of lights seen on the object, including three white circular ones that were evenly spaced straight across along the rear underside.

The witness also noticed two bluish rectangular configurations which he felt may have been an exhaust system on the back of the object. The object made a slight sound similar to the low growl of a high-performance sports car.

Daylight Silver Sphere Enters Cloud
February 24, 2017

At 3:05 PM, witness was near Sutersville and noticed a lot of contrails in the sky. He observed an aircraft moving NW far off in the sky. The aircraft was moving behind a cloud. The man watched as the aircraft exited the cloud and continued on.

Suddenly, he noticed an object in the sky that was not as high in altitude as the aircraft. The object seemed to just appear and was about twenty degrees off the horizon. The object looked like a bright silver sphere. "It was plain as day". The object moved slowly along the path behind the cloud where the aircraft had entered.

The object entered the cloud but never exited from it. The witness continued to watch for the object for several minutes but never saw the object again. The entire observation lasted about five seconds.

Did You Observe Something Strange During the Westmoreland County Air Show?
June 24-25, 2017

Screen capture from video used with permission of the witness

The fantastic 2017 Westmoreland County Air Show (PA) took place on June 24-25th at the Arnold Palmer Airport located in Latrobe. A few days later, I was contacted and shown a short video taken on Sunday afternoon during the airshow when the Blue Angels were doing their amazing demonstration. The witness had gone to the area to see the performance of the F-18 Hornets and was positioned near Whitney, just a short distance from the airport.

The witness videotaped the F-18 demonstration and later went home to review what he had recorded. He recalled that four of the Blue Angels had flown over his head and he followed them until they went out of sight. He then focused on a single F-18 moving in the opposite direction. As he watched the video, something odd appeared that he did not see when he was recording the event. A short segment of the video footage shows a dark object in the vicinity of the single aircraft.

CREEPY CRYPTIDS

The device used to take the video was a phone with low resolution. The video and photo still capture from it were examined by researcher Jim Brown who has had a lot of experience working with photo analysis of other alleged UFO and Paranormal photos and videos.

As determined in Jim's report, the most likely explanation is that the object is some type of balloon. It is my understanding, however, that the airspace around the airport was restricted during the time that the airshow was active, and no aircraft or other devices should have been in the vicinity.

I would be interested to know if anyone else attending the airshow observed, photographed, or videotaped anything unusual in the area that weekend. I can be contacted at 724-838-7768 or via email at: paufo@comcast.net.

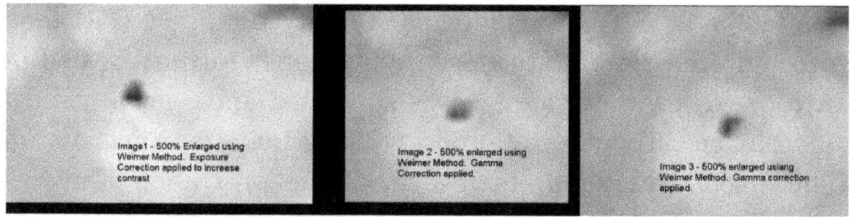

Photo enhancements of object from Jim Brown analysis. Used with permission of witness and Jim Brown

The following is Jim Brown's Report:

Analysis of Video of Unknown Airshow Object

The video was received as an MP4. It shows a plane passing in front of a cloud. Near the plane is an unknown object that appears to fade into the cloud as the plane passes. The object does not change position relative to the cloud while the image follows the plane across the cloud. Resolution is low; no definitive detail can be observed in the original video clip.

A camera anomaly (dead pixels, etc.) can be ruled out since the object follows the cloud as the camera is shifted. This also applies to lens flare as the object remains stationary with respect to the background even as the camera pans across the cloud.

In an attempt to resolve detail, I first applied an enlargement to three screen (frame) captures. This was done using the Weimer method to minimize pixelization. The detail appears to shift slightly, the first image shows a darker area at the bottom of the object while later images lose this effect becoming more uniform in nature.

Since resolution is low this effect may be due to relative position of the object as it hits each frame. MP4 Compression of the image may account for the effect adjacent pixels have on the image.

The triangular effect seen in the first screen capture is a result of the low resolution. This is common when pixels are triggered by surrounding ones. One can also see this effect when viewing the video and noting how the object appears to change shape from frame to frame as it approaches those adjacent pixels.

I also did a multi-frame overlay using a pixel weight scan in an attempt to compensate for the low-resolution issue. The numeric value of each pixel in the field containing the object was overlaid and averaged. Nine frames were used in this operation. The result indicated a pattern that would apply to a spherical shape, although no detail was resolved. The lower center of the sphere appears darker than the upper portion by 30%.

This would match what would be expected based on an object in that position illuminated by overhead sunlight.

Coloration was neutral; the object appears to be very dark or black based on pixel weighted values.

Conclusions based solely on the visual appearances in the video are speculative at best. The pattern matches what would be expected if the object was a small balloon, although due to the airshow in progress airspace was restricted. Whether this is a possibility would need to be verified by air traffic control at the show.

Jim Brown — Independent Research Associate
http://www.jimsdestinations.com/

Circle of Lights Over the Youngstown Side of Chestnut Ridge August 3, 2017

This encounter occurred on the Youngstown side of the Chestnut Ridge. It was just after midnight when the witness, who was lying in bed watching TV, noticed a bright light through a window up in the woods. The wooded area from the house is about one hundred twenty feet away, and the lights were over the woods about one hundred feet above the trees. The woods are very thick, and there was a slight breeze moving the trees.

The lights were behind the trees up on a hill and shining through the trees. She could see them as the trees were moving. First, she saw three bright perfectly round individual lights. The lights were quite large for that distance and appeared bright white with an orange tint. The lights were flat, and translucent, not clear like a spotlight.

The lights were positioned in a circle, kind of like in an arch or "like a string of pearls." As the trees moved, she believed she saw a total of five lights. They moved over the top of the trees and moved to her right towards the town of Youngstown when she lost sight of them.

She said the lights were larger and brighter than any star or Venus and did not have a beam or did not reflect on the surroundings. The total observation time was about five minutes. She thought about getting a camera to take a picture but didn't want to turn on any lights.

The witness ran from window to window in the house to get a look at a different. The witness had never seen anything like this before. She recalled there thinking, "What the heck is this? There was no sound" and remembered thinking, "It's so quiet." The woods are generally noisy with insect sounds, but there was no sound at all. She also thought it was odd that dogs in the area were not barking.

UFO Sighting Near Sutersville, PA
January 26, 2018

A UFO sighting was reported on the evening of January 26th near Sutersville in Westmoreland County. The witness noticed something odd in the sky over the river. What he saw were four round lights in a row. There were two very bright white lights in the center which were non-blinking. On each end was a bright green light that also did not blink.

The four large bright lights gave the impression they were attached to something. However, the witness could not see any silhouette. What he saw appeared quite large and moved steadily across the sky until the lights were lost as they passed over a hill.

UFO Observed During the Afternoon Over a House
May 14, 2018

The witness was in her home located in a rural area of Greene County. The woman was closing a window as a storm was approaching the area. As she looked through the window, she noticed a dark, hat-like saucer shaped object that was stationary over a neighbor's home about one hundred fifty feet away.

The object, while dark in color, was not quite black. It was estimated at twenty to twenty five feet in length and approximately eight to ten feet high. The witness did not observe any windows, lights, or sound. Toward the top of the object, there seemed to be some type of yellow or gold markings.

While the witness watched, the object banked and moved off into the sky toward the southeast, then just vanished from sight. The entire observation lasted six to ten seconds.

UFO Sightings Reported Over Cambria County September 2018

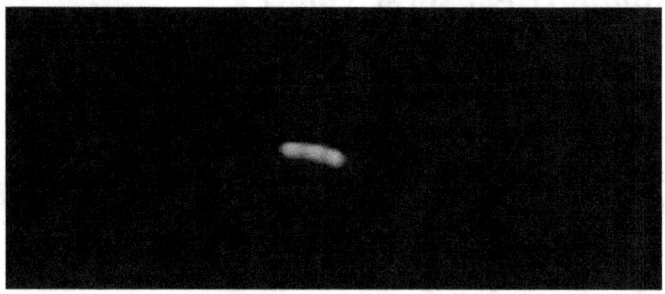

Photo used with permission of the witness

During September of 2018, a number of UFO sighting reports originated from Cambria County in Pennsylvania. Reports from observers were originating from locations between Johnstown and Ebensburg. Many of the reports were of unusual lights in the sky, and what was observed was not typical of navigational lighting on aircraft. A witness reported an object that hovered in place, and then within seconds would quickly jet across the sky to another location.

Other people in the area reportedly observed a V-shaped object with three separated lights. A photograph taken by a local resident is similar to what was reported.

On another occasion during daylight hours, an object that looked like a metallic sphere was observed making unusual maneuvers in the sky. While under observation, the object seemed to suddenly vanish within seconds, as though attempting to become invisible. At that point, the witness could see the outline of the object and could see through it. While this was occurring, the object was zigzagging to different locations in the sky at a very fast pace.

In mid-September during the early morning, another witness taking a walk near Colver, PA, observed a white oval shaped object moving slowly across the sky and vanish into the clouds. The object wasn't seen again.

Black Sphere Hovers Over Trees During Snowstorm in Fayette County
January 24, 2019

This report was submitted by Researcher Jim Brown and was used with his permission.

> Report was received at 11:00 AM, 24 January 2019.
>
> Witness contacted me via e-mail.
>
> Location of sighting: near Hopwood, Pa.
>
> Time of sighting: 9:30 AM
>
> Point of observation: Outdoors while clearing snow from porch steps.
>
> Weather conditions: Snowing moderately
>
> Description of event as derived from both initial report and phone
>
> Conversation: e-mail: I was clearing the snow from my front steps and noticed what looked to be a black ball hovering in the sky. It was over the trees in front of the house

and just seemed to be floating there. What was strange was that it was growing larger but not moving closer.

It just sat there in the sky for about 2 minutes. I tried to take a picture with my phone but as soon as I got the phone out snow had hit the camera lens and the picture blurred out. The ball then slowly began moving away and also was shrinking in size. It hadn't gone very far then it just shrank out of sight. That was the last I saw of it. I watched it for no more than about 5 minutes.

Additional details obtained by questioning on the phone: 24 January, 2019, 2:00 PM

The witness describes the object as a very black ball or sphere with no other details observed. It was about twice the apparent size of a full moon when at its largest size. When asked what drew his attention to it, he said it was just there when he looked up. He could not say if it was there prior to his first seeing it since he had just gone outside. He could not say how it first appeared in the sky.

I asked about how far away it was and based on the fact it was snowing moderately at the time and the witness statement that the object was clearly visible it was determined that it was within about 300 feet of his point of observation. Beyond that the snow would have obscured his view.

There was no sound associated with the sighting. The attempt to photograph the object was prevented likely by a snowflake hitting the camera lens and causing the image to be blocked. He described the picture he did obtain and said it was streaked / blurred and nothing could be identified. (Witness will make the picture available and I will attempt to verify the snowflake hypothesis as to why it failed to show.)

He said the object remained motionless for about two minutes then very slowly moved about 45 degrees horizontally above the trees, remaining visible the entire time. It should be noted that assuming the distance of 300 feet and the distance covered by the motion of the object, its speed would have been a matter of a few feet per second.

However, at that speed the size reduction could not be accounted for based on the distance, and had the motion been away from the point of observation, snow falling would have obscured visibility before the object was out of sight. Thus, it is apparent the actual size of the object was changing until it was too small to be seen, not a factor of it moving away from the observer.

The witness reported no other effects, and no negative or positive emotional aspects. He had no inclination as to what it was and made no claims of UFO or other speculations. He did go out and investigate around the trees, nothing physical was found. At his location it would not be expected any other witnesses would have also observed it, however he will check with neighbors and if they too saw something. He will pass along my contact information.

Update 28 January, 2019. I did receive the image he made, and nothing is visible. I can concur with what we determined earlier though; the image is distorted as a result of what appears to be water on the lens. One can only see varied blotches of light and dark to the extent the trees appear as dark areas on the lower portion of the image. There is no sign of the object, nor any detail of anything that might be in the area above the trees.

No further work expected on this case unless additional data is received.

CREEPY CRYPTIDS

Low Level UFO Encounter With Strange Electronic and Animal Effects Reported Near the Chestnut Ridge June 4, 2019

On the evening of June 4, 2019, two people were traveling near the Youngstown side of the Chestnut Ridge not far from Latrobe in Westmoreland County, Pennsylvania. The sky was clear with good visibility. The passenger in the car suddenly yelled out, "What are those lights?" The driver was watching the road and didn't notice them until they were pointed out.

The passenger was confused about what she was seeing since it looked so unusual. She saw what appeared to be a glass tube cylinder among bright lights that seemed to be covered with a smoke or haze. The cylinder appeared to be attached to a large V-shaped object with several rows of different colored lights.

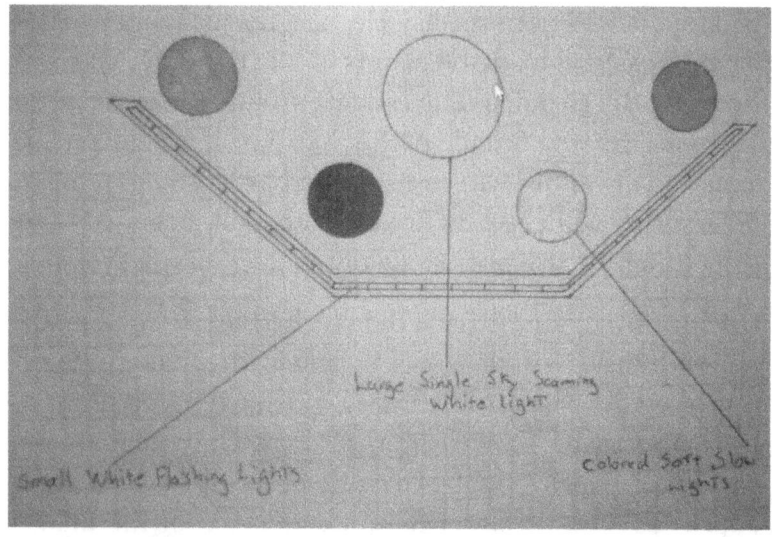

Sketch of the object drawn by one of the witnesses. Used with permission of the witness.

The driver pulled the car over and stopped the vehicle so he could view what the other person was watching. The man said he was amazed when he looked up and noticed the odd sight in the sky approximately eighty to one hundred yards away from the vehicle.

Hovering about sixty feet over the trees was a very strange looking object in the shape of a V. The V-shape was made up of numerous small rectangular shaped white lights. These lights were glowing but would brighten and dim at times. The driver estimated that there could have been fifty or more lights. The object was estimated to be about forty to fifty feet long.

This is a photo of a section of the Chestnut Ridge near where the object was observed.

Above the smaller lights were four larger round lights that were strobing and orange, blue, red, and green in color. The brightness of these colors appeared pale compared to the smaller rectangular white lights. These lights seem to strobe from left to right. There was a larger light that produced a beam that was scanning the sky above the object.

The driver lowered the windows as they continued to watch the object. The two observers were amazed that the hovering object was completely silent. As the witnesses continued to watch the object, some odd effects took place. The driver stated that it was as though "the electronic system of the car was having a seizure."

The radio was off at the time. However, they suddenly began to hear an odd clicking sound inside the vehicle, but they were unable to locate the source. At the same time, it was noticed that the dash lights were dimming on and off with the beat of the clicking sound. The driver also stated that soon after he was having a problem with his cell phone dropping the signal several times.

The observers watched the object for about three minutes and became very disturbed by the encounter, so he decided to leave the area and continue down the road. The passenger stated, "We were beside ourselves in awe". They didn't even think of trying to take a picture.

The object was still hovering as they began to drive down the road going about thirty miles per hour. That is when something else strange occurred. About thirty seconds after they left the location of the observation, a deer ran out from the woods in front of their car. The driver of the car is an experienced outdoorsman and said the deer looked dazed and confused. It was moments later that another deer did the same thing. Then just a short distance down the road, a bird hit the car windshield and continued on. As they continued for another short distance, an even stranger animal encounter took place.

The driver, who is very familiar with the native animals around the area, saw a creature that startled him. He said this creature stopped about 7 feet in front of his vehicle. This creature was directly in his headlights and he got a good look at it. He knew what it was, but the animal has been declared extirpated in Pennsylvania for many years.

He is certain he saw a wolverine. The animal looked directly at the vehicle and was about four feet long from tail to snout. It had light brown hair with dark spots with tufts of tan and white hair. It had its mouth open and showed its teeth before running off. Its body was thicker than the fishers that have been seen around this area. The witness said he was dumbfounded. As they continued on, more deer quickly exited the woods.

The driver commented, "all of these animals seemed confused and frightened. They were all crossing the road as to evade something that had scared them. I was in a state of amazement at what we encountered. I'll never forget that strange night."

Addendum: In 2020, another witness contacted me who provided information that he also saw this object at very close range and just a few miles away from where the original sighting took place on the same night.

When I began in the field investigations of UFOs and other phenomena in 1965, it became apparent that many UFO sightings could be explained as natural or man-made in origin. However, every year I receive UFO reports from across Pennsylvania that are not so easily explained away.

During my over 60 years of research, I have investigated multitudes of low-level UFO incidents where large, structured objects were observed at very close range. Many of these incidents occurred in daylight and were observed by more than one witness. These detailed close range UFO encounters have continued to occur in more recent years.

Southwestern Sections of Pennsylvania. Many Reports of Maneuvering Strange Lights High in the Sky July-October 2019

Beginning in July and continuing through October of 2019, I was receiving widespread reports from such areas as Ligonier, Mount Pleasant Township, and Delmont where observers at night were seeing bright light sources high in the sky. At times these bright objects hovered, made loops, and zig-zagged. On occasion, more than one object would join another object in the sky then would take off at a high rate of speed.

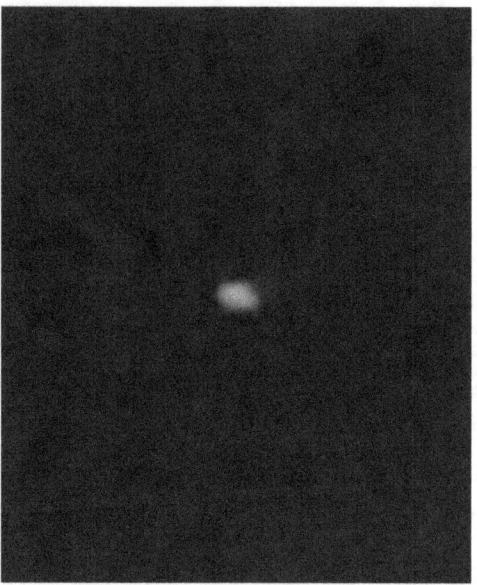

Photograph used with permission of the witness

The photograph above was taken on the evening of October 20, 2019, outside of Ligonier. The object appeared relatively low and moved up and down in the sky. The bright white object wobbled as it moved across the sky.

The witness believed the object was spherical or pill shaped. The objects that have been seen in the area recently also appear at times to have a dot in the center.

The witness couldn't be certain on the shape, and there could be some distortion from the focusing of the camera.

Stan Gordon

Four Black Spheres Enter Unusual Cloud in Fayette County, PA August 15, 2019

The following report was submitted by PA Paranormal Researcher Jim Brown.

> This daylight UFO incident is among numerous other UFO reports that have been reported in past weeks and months in Pennsylvania. The sighting occurred east of the Chestnut Ridge.
>
> Date: 08-15-2019
>
> Time: About 4:30 PM
>
> Location: Near Markleysburg, PA (Fayette County, PA)
>
> Witness name: (Withheld but on file)
>
> Weather conditions: Cloudy earlier but clear at the time. Temperature in the 70s.
>
> I was contacted via my website on 8-18-2019 and asked to call the Witness, regarding a strange thing he saw in the sky earlier in the week. The following narrative is based on this conversation which took place on 8-21-2019.
>
> The witness stated he had just gone outside for a break after doing some work in his basement. He had noticed how clear the sky was after earlier having a thundershower. What caught his attention was what he described as a black ball about the size of a full moon that came out of the northwest and flew into a puffy white cloud. He noticed that was the only cloud in the sky at the time. The total time the ball was seen was only a couple seconds.
>
> He called his wife to come out so he could tell her what he saw. Both were on the porch looking at the cloud. About 5 minutes later two more black balls appeared. One came out

of the east, the other slightly south of east. About 2 seconds passed between their appearances. They also flew into the cloud and disappeared. Both witnesses saw these two objects. Both objects moved about the same speed as the first one.

His wife went into the house to get a camera in case more appeared. While she was gone just a few seconds, a fourth object came out of the west and entered the cloud. This one was larger than the other ones. It also had four spikes sticking out of each side of it. These seemed to expand and shrink, possibly because the ball was rotating as it flew. Like the others it went into the cloud. Almost as soon as it entered, the cloud turned a slightly yellow color then seemed to just "wash itself out of the sky".

His wife had returned with the camera, but by the time she got there all that was left of the cloud was what looked like rain coming down below it. The rain seemed to evaporate before it reached the ground. There was no sign of any of the black objects. He attempted to take a picture but all that was apparent was the tree line and blue sky.

He watched the sky for some time but saw nothing more. Some clouds appeared after a while, but these were just normal cumulus clouds forming over the mountains as is common this time of day. No other effects were noted, no sounds or other abnormal weather conditions. Later that night there was another rain shower.

Cigar Shaped UFO Reports in Cambria County October 2019

On the evening of October 3, 2019, a series of UFO encounters began in Cambria County near Johnstown. Witnesses near South

Fork reported seeing a large metallic cigar shaped object with many bright lights moving very low above the ground.

Later that evening, another report came in from the Nanty Glo area. A witness reported seeing a cigar shaped object that looked metallic and was completely illuminated and very bright. The object seemed to be about sixty to seventy feet long and was moving through an area of fog. The object began to fade in and out and alternated from very bright to dim then just vanished from sight. Over the next week, other UFO sightings were reported from around the same area.

Two UFOs That Entered Clouds but Didn't Exit June 25, 2020

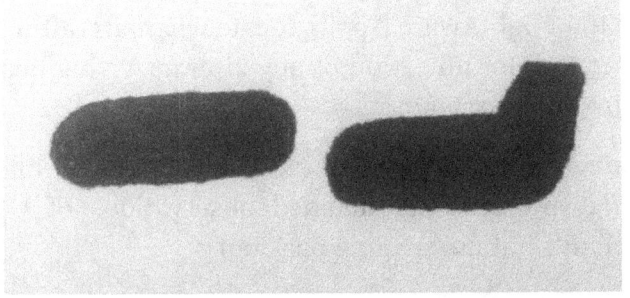

Sketch of the two cylindrical objects used with permission of the witness.

In late June 2020, a man taking photographs of the beautiful sunset observed something odd in the sky that still has him baffled. The sighting took place in a rural location not far from Murrysville, Pennsylvania. The witness was looking north when he noticed what seemed to be a jet airliner that suddenly appeared. The man grabbed his camera thinking that the jet with the sunset would make a nice picture.

As the man continued to watch, he realized that the shape of the jet looked unusual. He then realized that he was looking at two separate dark objects that were flying very close, but not at a level altitude. The object in front appeared to be slightly higher than the second object. The objects looked like two cylinders, similar to a fuselage with no wings that were dark, offset, and silent.

The second object had what looked like a vertical tower or tail section on it. There were no navigational lights on either object and no sound was heard while the objects were being observed. The objects were only seen for several seconds before the objects entered the tip of a slender long cloud.

The photographer grabbed his 35mm camera to have it ready to take a picture of the objects when they exited the cloud. He stood there watching for twenty minutes but the objects were never seen again. The cloud eventually faded away.

While the man continued to watch the sky, he called a friend who searched the FlightAware App to locate what aircraft were in the area. He found no indication of any aircraft having been in that area during the past hour.

Addendum: In more recent years, I have received information concerning several other detailed observations of UFOs that entered clouds but never came back out.

Large Spherical Object Moves Low Over Witness Near Irwin
July 11, 2020

The evening of July 11, 2020 was nice and comfortable, and the sky was clear, so a man decided to take one of his dogs for a walk. The man lived in the Irwin area only a few miles from the Turnpike. Suddenly, the witness heard the sound of multiple dogs barking loudly and running down the street where he lived. This was unusual. The situation was odd enough that the man took his dog back home, grabbed a flashlight and walked out to the backyard then moved toward the front of the house.

He could still hear numerous dogs barking from around the area. He stood on the street for about a minute trying to figure out where the dogs were located. He walked up the street a short distance and happened to look up into the sky in the northwest. That is when he noticed a circular object that seemed quite large, that appeared to be rising from the ground about a mile away. The object was glowing red and bright enough to make out the spherical shape.

The object traveled toward the east then turned southeast in his direction and moved steadily while maintaining the same altitude. The object was now only about five to six houses away from where he was standing and only about two hundred feet off the ground. The object, whatever it was, remained completely silent while under observation. The witness didn't have his phone with him to take a picture.

The witness described the object as circular or egg shape. It was about twenty to thirty feet in diameter- the size of a small house. There was a pulsating red glow emitting from the object with a rhythm similar to that of a heartbeat. While the object had a definite shape, it appeared to be semi-transparent. One section of the object appeared to be a darker color than the others. There were, also what appeared to be circuit board lines going through some sections of the object as well.

CREEPY CRYPTIDS

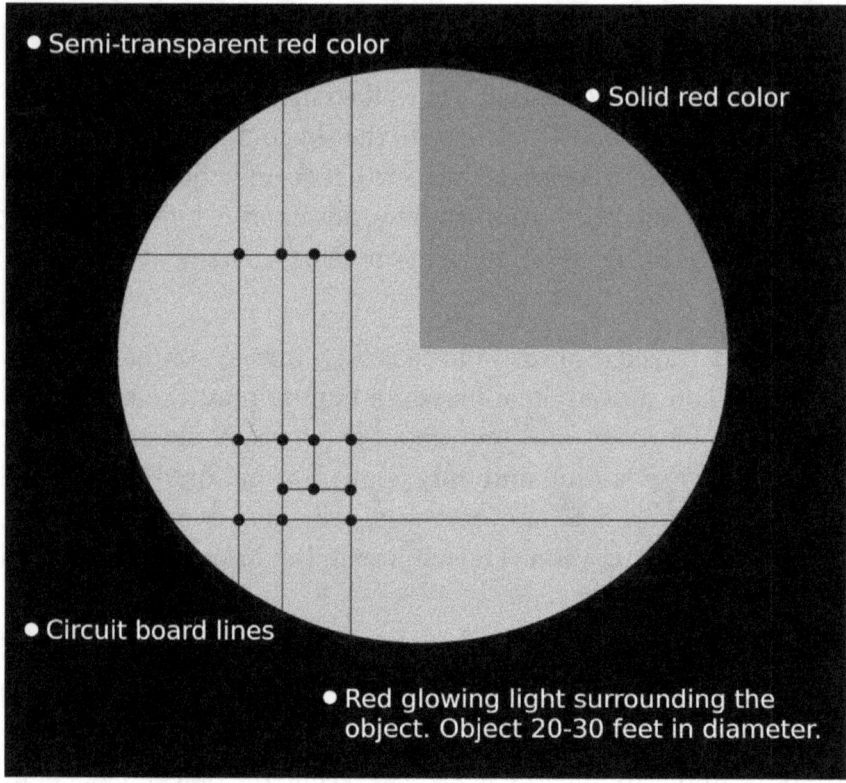

Graphic depiction of the object, used with permission of the witness.

The object was just about to move over the head of the man when he was distracted by the loud barking of more dogs running near him on the street. He was concerned that they might bite him, and he was focusing on them. He was about forty feet from his home and could hear his two dogs barking as well.

Seconds later the barking suddenly stopped and there was the sound of silence. Seconds later he looked back to the object which now was positioned directly above him, but it was now about one thousand feet in altitude.

The object moved from his property and over his neighbor's moving toward the east. He ran behind his house to see where the object was going but his vision was blocked by the trees in that area.

Addendum: There have been numerous UFO encounters reported for years throughout the Irwin and North Huntingdon areas. This sighting is among a number of other UFO sightings that have been reported in recent weeks from this area of the state and elsewhere.

Creepy Cryptids

Stan Gordon

Chapter Two

Close Encounters with Mini-UFOs

When descriptions of UFOs are discussed, many of the observations have been described as discs, triangular, cigar, and even rectangular shaped objects in the sky. Since the 1960s, I have been investigating what I have called "Mini-UFOs". These objects are rarely discussed in the literature and are most intriguing.

Those smaller objects have been reported approaching close to individuals, tapping on the windows of homes, and pacing and entering vehicles. They have entered houses through open windows. They have suddenly appeared inside of homes and sometimes exit through a wall or open window.

They have appeared during the daylight as well as night and don't seem to be affected by weather conditions. They have been encountered in populated urban areas as well as rural locations. Investigators of hauntings and ghost sightings often talk about their observations with similar small spheres of lights or what they often refer to as orbs.

These smaller objects generally range in size from a few inches to about one to two feet in diameter. While commonly spherical, other configurations have been reported as well. These objects are sometimes solid and look metallic. In other cases, they are just light sources of various intensities. There are cases reported that describe the objects as transparent or translucent.

These encounters have continued to be reported including in more recent years. The following are some of the interesting cases that have come to my attention.

Two Boys Thought They Were Under Attack by Small Metallic Sphere
Spring of 1966

This incident took place during the Spring of 1966, in Ohio Township, a suburb of Pittsburgh, Pennsylvania. There were two brothers involved ages fourteen and sixteen at the time. It was about 7 AM that beautiful morning when their father took the boys outside to do chores.

The man was showing the boys how to properly weed his garden to prepare the area for planting tomatoes. It was a large area, and it was going to take quite a while to complete that task. The boys' father had left for work and the young fellows continued to hoe the soil. The older brother, whom I interviewed about this incident, had noticed something moving very low near some trees and a power line in the distance.

He first saw the object about two hundred yards away across a field and only about four feet above the ground. His first thought was that it was a balloon, so he really didn't pay much attention to it. He never pointed it out to his brother at that time. The object moved at a steady pace following the terrain and moving in their direction.

A short time later, the older brother happened to look up again and the strange spherical object was now approaching closer to them. That was when he called out to his brother to get his attention for him to look at the mysterious object that was now only about thirty five feet away. That is when the round, dull-gray metallic sphere suddenly stopped.

One of the fellows commented to me that their first thought was that they were under attack. They both responded by grabbing a handful of dirt balls and throwing them at the object. He didn't think they actually hit it, but the object then began to move away, back toward the direction from where it originated from.

When the object was very low and close by it looked like a "giant ball bearing." It was about eight inches in diameter and looked like it was made of solid metal. It was perfectly silent. The witness told me that they really didn't fear the object but realized it was something unusual. The entire encounter lasted about one to two minutes.

Small Luminous Sphere Seen at Close Range Near Derry
July 2010

A man had been taking his daily exercise and was walking around the area around 9 PM when his attention was drawn to a luminous object. The object, which was estimated to be about fifteen feet above the ground, looked solid and round, about two inches in diameter, and of a pale white color.

The slow-moving object approached to as close as about fifteen feet from the observer. The witness said he thought the object might hit some trees, but it just moved around them and continued to move out of sight until it was gone.

Small Rectangular UFO Close to the Ground in Mount Pleasant Township
August 12, 2010

About 9:30 PM, a witness was watching the clear sky hoping to see a meteor, but instead observed something stranger. The witness described an object that was rounded in the front and extended back about eight to nine feet long in a rectangular shape.

The entire object was about fifteen inches high and glowed with a soft white color. The object seemed to be only about fifteen feet distance from the porch and about three feet from the ground. It stayed still for about two minutes, then moved off. A short time later two lights were seen over some nearby trees.

Small Red Object Low to the Ground Near the Chestnut Ridge
November 24, 2010

At about 6:10 PM, on the Youngstown side of the ridge, two men were standing outside when one of them noticed a red spherical shaped object about sixty yards away in a wooded area.

The witnesses, startled by what they were seeing, ran closer towards the object, but one man stopped about halfway and would not approach closer. One observer described the object, which was stationary at the time, stating that it looked somewhat like, "a ball with the top quarter cut off".

The witness explained that it was if the top quarter of the orb was cut off but was still slightly dome shaped. The object was flat on the bottom. The object appeared to be about sixty to seventy two inches long, and about thirty to thirty six inches high. The object was red in color, but non-glowing with a thin white colored bottom and a yellow edge that was located between the top of the orb and the bottom.

While the one witness stood about seventy feet from the motionless object, he noticed some sort of "static discharge" or white spark coming from the bottom white section. The witness remained motionless as the object slowly moved away from his position. The object then made some changes in direction and finally, with great speed, it moved over a hill and vanished from sight. The object was silent and was never more than three to four feet above the ground. The observation lasted about fifteen seconds.

Three Small Glowing Circular Lights Rise From the Ground
April, 2012

This incident occurred in a rural area of Forest County and took place at about dusk. The witness was out looking for her cats when she noticed something odd about fifty feet north of the center of the driveway. Suddenly, the berm of the road started to glow in a circular shape. She observed a circle of white light that was about two feet in circumference.

As she watched, the glowing circle became brighter and began to rise off the ground to a height of about six feet. The object then formed into a dome shape with what was described as strands of smoke that were swirling inside the lighted circle and appeared to look somewhat like a jellyfish. The object then began to slowly move off toward a nearby field at which time it began to fade away until it could no longer be seen.

About five minutes later, the witness noticed a second similar glowing circular object about thirty feet away from where the first object was observed. The object looked the same as the first one and followed the same pattern. It got brighter, rose off the ground, and moved towards the field and vanished.

This was followed by a third similar object and doing the same actions. The third luminous circle of light appeared in the middle of the road about sixty feet from the second observation point. The total observation times of the three anomalies was during a fifteen-minute span. No sound was heard during the sighting.

The witness commented that one cat ran from the field and wanted to go inside the house, which was unusual for that animal.

After the incident, the woman and her husband went to the locations where the objects were seen but they found nothing unusual. There was a slight breeze in the area at the time and the weather was clear.

Small Sphere Enters Moving Vehicle
July 30, 2012

It was about 5:00 pm on July 30, 2012, when an unusual incident occurred. A man was driving toward the east on Interstate 80 between Route 880 and U.S. 15 West near the town of Bloomsburg. There were no other vehicles in the vicinity of this driver, and he was moving at a good pace. The weather was clear with low humidity, so the driver was enjoying the ride with his windows down.

As the driver continued down the road, he began to experience an uneasy feeling as though something was wrong with his vehicle or that some type of accident was about to occur. He was trying to find a music station on his radio and was pushing the auto seek button. Then a short time later, something very strange took place which the motorist will never forget.

Suddenly, a white, translucent, round object, that appeared to be about the diameter of a soft ball appeared outside of the passenger side window. The object was not luminous.

The witness explained to me that the sphere may have been a little more oval than a soft ball in shape. It paced the vehicle as it moved, then floated into the cab through the open window. As the man watched, the object dropped slowly to the floorboard, then quite slowly moved towards the driver along the floor.

The witness was able to see through the sphere and noticed that the surface of the object appeared to be crisscrossed and divided by a line about one quarter of an inch wide. The man said looked similar to a vein that was darker than the object and somewhat of a gray color.

The man, concerned about what was happening, had taken his foot off the accelerator as he was concentrating more on the object then the roadway. The object moved very slowly along the floor, then proceeded up the hump in the middle of the floorboard. It then continued on to move toward the driver's feet.

When it reached his right foot, it suddenly stopped, then reversed direction until it became centered on the hump. The object then departed the truck by passing through the seat into the back of the cab, and then out the bed of the moving vehicle. The man could not see the object after that. The incident lasted totally about thirty to forty five seconds.

The witness commented that the object moved in a nonchalant manner and just seemed as though it came in to look around and didn't care that it was being seen. The mans' odd uneasy feeling went away when the object left the vehicle. The man also told me that there were no vehicles, signs, bridges, or anything that could have caused a reflection in that area.

Small Sphere Seen Through Window Near Masontown March 21, 2013

Investigated by J. Brown

Approximately 8:15 PM. The witness was sitting in his house watching TV with his son. The curtain on the window was open allowing a direct view outside. A light caught his attention coming from the window. He saw a light, best described as a small glowing ball through the glass. Both he and his son saw the light. It was about 6 feet from the window, in front of a large tree in the yard. His thoughts were that someone was in his yard shining a light into the window.

CREEPY CRYPTIDS

Fearing a possible break in or other intrusion he went to the den and armed himself with a gun and a flashlight before going out the side door to confront the intruder. His son continued to watch from inside. Upon turning the corner of the house, he shined his flashlight toward the ball of light. It immediately shot straight up into the sky and vanished. His son witnessed the same from inside the house.

Both witnesses were interviewed and gave the same account of the events. More in-depth questioning also brought out a few more details. The object was described as a solid, glowing sphere, not simply a light source.

No other detail could be seen, although both said it had well defined edges. It was about 10-12 inches in diameter based on comparison to the tree trunk diameter. The position was well below the horizon as seen from the window, thus confirming its nearby location.

When asked about how it moved both witnesses said it had little to no movement until it shot into the air. At that point it was still seen as a rapidly moving sphere, not a beam of light. Several branches of the tree extended above the object's location. Neither witness could definitively say whether it went through the branches or between them, however, both said the direction upward was direct with no discernible shift as it moved through the tree limbs.

Weather conditions were mostly cloudy, Temperature in the 30s at the time. No sound was heard, nor any other effects noted. No physical evidence was found after the sighting. A follow up contact 25 March 2013 provided no additional information.

Stan Gordon

Mini Light Configuration on Bed Near Witness
July 13, 2015

On the evening of July 13, 2015, a woman staying overnight at a friend's house had an unusual experience. The incident occurred in a rural area of Ligonier Township, Westmoreland County, PA, where many strange events have taken place over the years.

The encounter occurred sometime between 11:30 PM and midnight. The witness had just turned off the bedroom light. She had arranged the pillows and the comforter on the bed and was preparing to watch TV. A few minutes, later her eyes caught something only about two feet away on the comforter.

The woman couldn't figure out what she was seeing. Her first thought was that it was something, "like computer keys or a firefly". What she was looking at was a tiny light configuration totaling about one and one half inches in length. There were three rectangular lights all in a row and evenly spaced. They were translucent and bright yellow.

As the witness watched, a pattern of blinking began to occur. The light closest to her blinked one time. The middle light went out. The third light blinked once, the middle light then blinked, then it started back to the same pattern with the first light blinking once again.

The witness reached out to grab at the light configuration and touched it but felt nothing. When she made contact with it, the light configuration just vanished. She looked all around but it was not observed again. The witness had never experienced anything like that before and is puzzled by what she saw.

CREEPY CRYPTIDS

Mini-UFO Hovers Near Window, Ligonier Area
September 20, 2017

This incident occurred on September 20, 2017, in the Ligonier area, not far from the Chestnut Ridge. The witness was in bed when she noticed a light outside the window during the early morning hours. There were no lights in that area of the property. She got up and went to the window. Suspended in the air was an illuminated object about six to seven feet from the window and about eight to nine feet above the ground. The object was hovering and moved around a little from left to right.

The object was small and about the diameter of a silver dollar. The color of the object was described as yellowish and pale green. The light was steady but did not glow brightly. It did not emit any light that reflected on the surrounding area. The object was not completely round but appeared as a flattened circle and more egg shaped. On the left side, there was a small section missing (a dark spot) kind of like a wedge of a pie where no light was emitted from. No sound was heard.

Haystack Shaped Mini-UFO Glides Over the Ground Near Fayette City
October 2017

A mini-UFO encounter took place in late October near Fayette City, PA, in Fayette County. Early that morning, a man went outside to warm up his wife's car. As he walked down the steps he looked toward her car and saw something only about ten to twelve feet away by the right bumper. The lights were on and the area around the car was well illuminated.

Stan Gordon

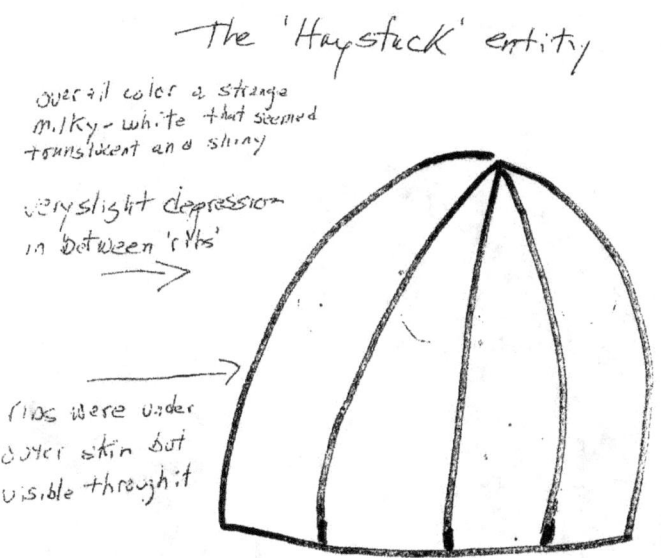

Graphic depiction of the object, used with permission of the witness.

The witness said he saw an object that was about two feet tall and shaped like a haystack. The object was translucent, and shiny, and a milky-white color. There were vertical ribs that seemed to be the superstructure that looked like chrome straws that could be seen through the translucent structure.

The object, which was silent, was gliding one to two inches off the ground and was motionless when he first saw it. Whatever the object was, after several seconds it must have realized that the witness had approached until he reached about six feet from it.

It suddenly zoomed extremely fast across the driveway to the left side of the car, then made a perfect right angle turn along the driver's side of the car into the dark and was not seen again. The entire incident lasted only seconds.

The witness wished he had his cell phone with him so he could have taken a picture. The witness has no idea what he saw but feels that it may have been some type of a probe.

CREEPY CRYPTIDS

Small Sphere on the Ground Blocks Motorist
November 8. 2019

Graphic depiction of a small spherical object based on eyewitness accounts.

One of my research associates, Jim Brown from Fayette County, PA (www.jimsdestinations.com) received an interesting account of a small sphere that was on the ground and blocking a roadway during the mid-afternoon. Here is Jim's report:

> About 4:30 PM I received a call from a nearby witness who is aware I investigate unusual events. A transcript of his narrative follows:
>
> "I was coming home from Masontown on the Bowood Road. As I went over the top of a rise, I saw this ball in the

road just sitting there. It was about 2 feet across and was blocking the road. I couldn't get around it, so I stopped.

I sat there for a minute then decided to get out and move it so I could continue home. I even thought about taking it home as an oddity. But when I opened the car door it started to just fade away. Not quick. It took a few seconds to vanish. But then it disappeared. It never moved, just faded away. I closed the door and wondered, what the hell was that? After that I just went on home, nothing else to say."

I asked a few questions and got some additional information. He said the object was silvery gray in color. No details, just a sphere about 2 feet in diameter. He could not recall if there was a shadow under it. (Weather was mostly cloudy but still should have caused a darkening under the object.) He stopped about 50 feet away from the object. Beyond that he had no other details to report. No physical evidence was seen or obtained. A few leading questions provided no additional reliable information. Limited data, no other witnesses present.

Strange Orbs of Light Seen in Areas of Bigfoot Activity

I have discussed elsewhere in this book the subject of what I have called "Mini-UFOs" that I have been investigating since the 1960s. Those smaller generally spherical luminous objects have been reported approaching close to individuals, tapping on the windows of homes, and entering vehicles and structures through open windows.

They have suddenly appeared inside of homes and sometimes exit through a wall or open window. They have appeared during the daylight as well as night and they don't seem to be affected by weather conditions. They have been encountered in populated urban areas as well as rural locations. Investigators of hauntings and ghost sightings often talk about their observations with similar small spheres of light.

It was during the spring and summer of 1972, when some odd activity began to be reported by residents living along Humphrey Road outside of Greensburg came to my attention. There was a large, wooded area that had always been peaceful with just the normal wildlife sounds. Then it began- loud screams and cries emanated from that area. Strange large footprints began to show up on by local homes, and something large and bipedal was heard stomping through the foliage.

Sightings of a tall and broad-shouldered creature in the same area began to be reported. During that time, local residents were also reporting seeing strange luminous activity around their properties that they had never seen before. During one early morning in July, two witnesses saw two orange objects close to the size of a golf ball, meandering around some tree branches about eight feet above the ground. While the lights didn't blink, the witnesses said that they looked like giant fireflies.

In the years to follow, more cases of strange, illuminated objects associated with the Bigfoot phenomena came to my attention. During the massive Bigfoot outbreak during 1973, many very strange incidents were being reported across Pennsylvania. There were well documented cases of UFOs and Bigfoot observed together at the same time and place.

It was during that time period that a lot of Bigfoot activity was reported in the Derry Township area of Westmoreland County. A family at one farm reported that a Bigfoot had made several return visits to the property. They had heard its screams and had seen it. One person commented that maybe it was just a coincidence but soon after they saw or heard the creature, a red tubular object would pass over the property and illuminate the ground below it.

During September of 1973 north of Pittsburgh, two witnesses watched as a seven to eight feet tall Bigfoot covered in white hair run across the road toward a wooded area. What made the encounter even stranger was that the creature was carrying a small ball of light in one of its hands. Soon after, an object appeared in the sky and projected a beam of light into the woods where the creature had entered.

I have heard many other reports since then of unusual light phenomena associated with Bigfoot activity in certain areas. I have talked with Bigfoot researchers from around the country as well as here in Pennsylvania who are aware of cases of small luminous spheres or other unusual light sources that have been seen around trees and low off the ground in locations that have a history of Bigfoot activity.

There are also cases where odd swarms of what appear to be oversized fireflies that actually illuminate the surrounding area have also been observed in locations where Bigfoot has been reported.

Eric Altman has spent years investigating Bigfoot sightings in Pennsylvania and he is often out in the woods trying to locate one of these elusive creatures. He has seen odd light phenomena on several occasions while conducting his research.

It was an evening in August of 2009 that Eric, along with a team of other Bigfoot investigators, decided to explore an area of Rockton Mountain located between Clearfield and Dubois. That forested area has had a long history of Bigfoot encounters and there had been some recent sightings reported.

Eric was equipped with a thermal FLIR night vision device, along with some other gear. The team had parked and were walking off in the distance to enter the woods. During the evening, a light was noticed from about four hundred yards away moving around their parked vehicles. The light was small yet bright and gave the impression that a person might be walking around and smoking a cigarette. The light, however, seemed to move back and forth and all around the cars.

Eric and another researcher became concerned and decided to walk toward the parking lot to see what was going on. According to Eric, they approached their vehicles and from about seventy five feet away and shined their flashlight beams toward the parking area, but no one was there. When they shined the beams in that area, the light suddenly went out.

They approached the area, but there was no one around. They looked around and under the parked vehicles, but everything was normal. About that time, the other researcher received a phone call. It was moments later that some stranger activity took place. A terrible odor similar to manure suddenly encompassed the area. They had no idea where it could have originated from.

Eric said that odd smell was followed by the sound of heavy footsteps walking away from that location into the foliage. Eric used his FLIR so he could look around in the dark, but they could not see what was creating the loud footfalls, and oddly the horrific smell dissipated as the sound of the heavy stepping moved away in the distance.

In October of 2009, Eric and a group of Bigfoot researchers returned to the Rockton Mountain area where reports of Bigfoot activity had continued. There were also accounts concerning large rocks being thrown toward hikers, and wood knocking sounds. That evening some of the investigators observed an odd luminous source in the woods ahead of them.

Eric told me that it looked like a flame in a lantern that was being swung around. Eric walked toward the light but as it got closer it suddenly would vanish. He returned to the campsite, but soon after the strange light reappeared again. Eric once again approached close to the light source which again just disappeared. They were never able to find a source for what they saw that evening.

In August of 2015, two experienced Bigfoot researchers had an unusual experience at Quebec Run Wilds in Fayette County located on the eastern edge of the Chestnut Ridge. There have been many Bigfoot encounters reported over the years in this general area. Dwayne Pintoff and Eric Altman were conducting some night investigations in the area. The following information was obtained from the report that Dwayne submitted on the occurrence.

The two men were listening to the sounds of cicadas, and that of some occasional wildlife from the surrounding woods. Dwayne and Eric sat on the back of their cars hoping to hear any sounds that might be related to some Bigfoot activity.

It was about 8:30 PM, and Dwayne was becoming bored so he decided to do a wood knock to see if he might receive any response. As he moved toward a tree, he noticed a bright orange-red glow in the distance. Dwayne didn't think much of the light thinking that it was likely some campers in that area.

It was a few minutes later that Dwayne realized that the light appeared to have moved closer and now appeared to have a spherical shape and seemed to have grown in size as well. He soon pointed it out to Eric who thought it was just a campfire or a beacon light. When Dwayne looked back a few minutes later the orange sphere was not visible.

That is when Dwayne noticed about one hundred yards away to their left, what he described as a maize yellow colored beam of light. Eric looked at that light and thought it could be someone with a glow stick looking for firewood or night hiking. Eric decided to take a short walk.

As Dwayne continued to watch he could tell that the light was actually rectangular in shape and was now moving in an erratic motion and was changing color from the maze yellow to a bluish-white color. The light soon moved out from the trees and backed deeper into a less dense tree line. The light was now moving along the ground then suddenly rose up about fifteen to twenty feet into the tree branches. This activity had taken place during about ten to fifteen minutes. Eric had just returned, and Dwayne mentioned that the light had been making some odd movements.

The two men moved toward the center of the road and continued to watch the object as it moved among the trees. It was only minutes later when the light appeared to be moving in their direction and came to about sixty feet from the two men. The object had now returned to the yellow color and had also changed from the rectangular shape to what now looked to be about a two-foot-long elongated object with a pointed top, pointed sides, and a longer pointed bottom. It gave the impression a luminous cross that was glowing/pulsating and the colors of the object were changing again.

The object seemed to move almost like a balloon although it was clearly not one. The bottom of the silent object appeared to be in a snake-like motion. Eric grabbed his military grade flashlight and shined the beam toward the mysterious luminous object.

As the beam from the flashlight struck the object, Dwayne said that a translucent bluish-white clear vortex or portal appeared then the object was suddenly absorbed in a bright flash, leaving behind a sparkling of electrically charged particles falling to the ground below. Suddenly, the surrounding area became dark once again. From Eric's vantage point, Eric told me, however, that he was only able to see the ball of light that just suddenly disappeared.

Both men were now startled by what they saw and had no idea what they had just seen. They sat there and discussed what had just happened and for ten to fifteen minutes kept looking to see if the light would appear again. They decided to walk over to the area where they had last seen it to see if there was any evidence. They were unable to find any physical traces related to what they had seen and after standing around that area for about thirty minutes, decided to return to their cars.

The strange events of that night weren't over. Soon after they reached their vehicles, Dwayne once again decided to try another tree knock. He started walking toward the tree where he had made the first tree knock. It was then that he noticed that reddish-orange glow again. The glow seemed to be increasing in size and getting closer. Dwayne called out to Eric that the light had returned and was moving in their direction.

The two men were standing together at this point so they both had the same view. They watched as the light approached to about one hundred yards away. This time, the object was about the size of a bowling ball and was a dark orange-red color. The object made a ninety degree turn to their right and ascended slowly over a rock covered hillside that that followed the terrain. It was then that the two observers decided to call it a night. The men have no idea what they encountered that night.

On page 91 of this book you will find the detailed report from my research associate Jim Brown concerning the May 10, 2016, close range Bigfoot encounter that occurred on Mud Pike near Fairchance. That location is only miles away from Quebec Run Wilds. During that incident, the creature actually put its hands on the front of a vehicle before running off toward the woods.

CREEPY CRYPTIDS

On the evening of May 13, 2016, a team of Bigfoot investigators went to the Mud Pike area to look for any evidence of the recent Bigfoot encounter. They set up several audio recorders in case any unusual sounds were heard. Later that evening, some odd white lights were seen in and around the trees.

What they saw looked like a large lightning bug or firefly about fifty yards into the forest. Eric Altman and another researcher who was there observed one large luminous object that looked like an over-sized lightning bug about the size of a golf ball and white in color.

They also observed what looked like a dull flashlight beam about fifteen to twenty feet up in a tree. Some of the other researchers also watched another white lighted object on the opposite side of the road that rose up and down and moved back and forth before departing. It was about thirty eight degrees at the time and quite cool in that mountainous area and generally too cold for lightning bugs.

In the days to follow, another group of Bigfoot researchers also visited the area, and during the event, they observed other odd light phenomena in the air including a swarm of what looked like over-sized fireflies that illuminated the surrounding area as they moved. One researcher, curious as to what he was seeing, began to approach the luminous objects, but they moved away in the distance as he got closer.

Stan Gordon

Chapter Three

Bigfoot Encounters

Small Bigfoot Leaps Onto a Moving Vehicle
Fall of 2012

A witness was nice enough to share a personal account with me that had occurred during the fall of 2012 in a rural area of Westmoreland County not far from the fairgrounds. As the driver was moving down the road, suddenly from the right side of the highway, a four foot tall hair covered creature jumped from the bank and jumped onto the hood of the car.

The creature remained there for only seconds than jumped off and ran down the road and out of sight. The witness had never seen any creature like this before and could only assume that it might have been a young Bigfoot.

Is Bigfoot Visiting Indiana County, PA?
January 2013

I have received information from a person who lives in a rural location of Indiana County that some odd happenings occurred around her home during the week of January 6, 2013. Most of the incidents seemed to occur during the early morning hours.

First, something was banging on the side of her house. In the days to follow, she began to hear a sound similar to a woman whining that seemed to be originating from outside and close to the house. One night, she caught a glimpse of a large figure outside of a window. Towards the later part of the week, the witness was outside and noticed a lot of deer tracks in the snow around her yard.

She also was surprised to see a series of small five toed footprints, which continued across a large section of her property. The tracks, which had a wide stride between them, were estimated to be about eight inches long, but unusually wide for a human. The toes were wide and rounded. The heels of the footprints were pressed deep in the snow. The woman wondered why a person would be walking bare foot in the snow.

Tracks Followed in Heavy Snow Just Stop in Cambria County February 2015

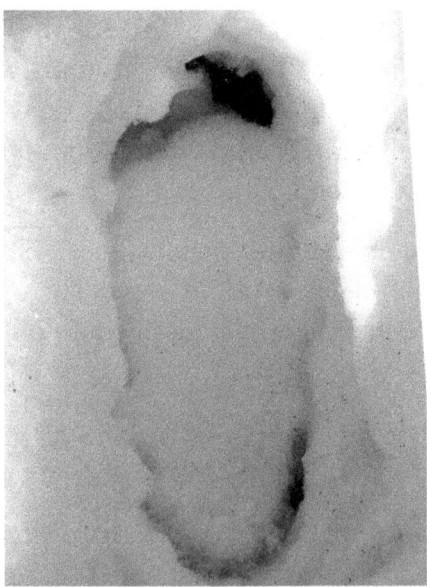

A picture of one of the tracks in the snow.
Used with permission of the witness.

This incident occurred in a wooded area near Beaverdale in Cambria County in February of 2015. The witness was taking a walk after a heavy deep snow had fallen. The person involved was up in the woods behind her house when she saw a series of large, unusual footprints.

A picture of some of the tracks in the snow that just stopped when there should have been more tracks. Used with permission of the witness.

The woman followed the tracks and noticed that the toes marked the surface of the snow as the foot pressed into the heavy snow. There were four apparent toes, but the ground conditions made it hard to determine if there was an additional toe. The witness didn't have anything with her to measure the tracks that were quite large and estimated to be about fourteen to fifteen inches in length. The tracks were narrow in width and were estimated to be about five inches wide or less toward the heel.

The stride between the tracks was quite extensive and at least four feet between the tracks. As the woman followed the footprints, they continued through an open area of the woods and walked over a large pile of tree cuttings and then continued off through the woods. There were dozens of tracks that went down off a hill at an angle and were followed for quite a distance.

As the trail of footprints continued toward a tree, they suddenly just stopped abruptly. It was an open area and there should have been more tracks. They suddenly ended as if whatever made them had just vanished. There has been a history of other possible Bigfoot activity in that general area. I have been receiving reports over the years of other similar footprints that are quite narrow in the width from other locations in the state.

Bigfoot Looks Into a Car at the Driver
April 17, 2016

I learned of another Bigfoot encounter when I was giving a presentation on UFOs and Cryptid reports. A woman and her daughter approached me and told me about an experience that the mother had on April 17, 2016. The witness, who was quite upset after the incident, called her daughter soon after it occurred. She gave her daughter a lot of details on the phone and her daughter proceeded to write them down.

Her daughter had brought her note pad along and shared that information with me. I had the chance to talk with the witness in detail and later that day, I went with the witness and another relative to the sighting location just a short distance outside of West Newton. I searched the immediate area, but nothing unusual was observed.

The incident occurred during the evening on a rural road just a short distance from West Newton. The woman was driving about thirty five miles per hour and traveling towards West Newton. As she drove along the stretch, on the passenger side of the road to her right, she saw a tall dark figure come out of a clearing and walk up on the road just as she was about to pass that area. She slowed down to look and saw the creature was at the passenger side of the car. What she saw stood approximately seven feet tall. It was covered with long brownish-red hair. The arms were long and skinny.

What frightened her the most were its large shiny red eyes that seemed to be luminous. The creature was looking into the passenger side window at her. The woman told me she was very frightened and hit the gas and sped down the road to get away from the creature. The witness mentioned that she doesn't like scary things and had no interest in Bigfoot or watching such TV programs about the creature. She also stated, "I never thought it would happen to me".

Addendum: The West Newton area and other nearby Westmoreland County communities have had a long history of Bigfoot encounters. In the late 1960s, local residents reported encountering the "Lowber Monster". A white hair covered creature was reported by locals and strange footprints were found.

Bigfoot Touches Vehicle in Fayette County, PA May 10, 2016

There have been continuous reports in past years of encounters with Bigfoot throughout many locations in Fayette County, PA. The earliest firsthand Bigfoot account I have on record dates back to 1931. Additionally, going back to the early 1970's, some of the strangest Bigfoot incidents on record occurred in this area. Many Bigfoot sightings continue to occur in this area, and quite often along or near the Chestnut Ridge.

On May 11, 2016, I received a phone call from Researcher Jim Brown who lives in Fayette County. Jim has been a long- time research associate of mine. He advised me that he had received an interesting report concerning two encounters with large hairy creatures. Jim wanted to see if I had received other reports. I had not received other reports from the date of the occurrence.

CREEPY CRYPTIDS

The following is the report Jim Brown has submitted on the case.

May 10, 2016. Hairy Creature Sightings, near Fairchance, PA on Mud Pike.

I received a phone call on the morning of 5-11-2016 reporting an incident that involved two "large hairy animals" on Mud Pike in Fayette County, Pa. This report covers the facts as reported in that case. (Witnesses have requested to remain anonymous, Name and address withheld). There were two witnesses in the vehicle, both interviewed separately, and details are in agreement with each other.

Weather conditions: Pouring rain, fog, Temperature about 52 degrees F.

Observations occurred from inside the vehicle that was involved in the incident. (Details follow)

Date / Time: 10 May 2016, Approximately 2300 hrs.

The following summary is based on both initial phone interview and personal interview with each witness. The witnesses were returning from visiting family on Chestnut Ridge on their way home. About halfway down Mud Pike the driver saw what appeared to be a large hairy animal cross the road walking upright.

He did not see it very clearly and could not rule out a bear walking on hind legs. But it did get his attention and he slowed to a crawl as he passed the area where he saw it. Using a flashlight, both witnesses were trying to catch a glimpse of it in the woods below. They did not see that creature again.

Suddenly a second creature came from the bank on the left into the path of their car about 20 feet ahead. The driver immediately slammed on his brakes and stopped with the creature clearly visible in the headlights about 10 – 15 feet in front of the car. Neither witness had a camera, so no photos were obtained.

I asked them to describe the creature. It was about 7 feet high, standing upright on two legs with arms well below the hips. It stared directly at the car, eyes glowing bright red. It was covered head to toe with long, black, or very dark hair. The hair was so long that no facial features besides the eyes could be seen.

The body also was covered to the point that no sexual features could be determined. Also noted were the palms of its hands which were hairless and black. No claws were seen. Feet were not seen as at the angle of view the hood of the car blocked the ability to see the ground at this close of a distance.

No smells or sounds were noted; however, the car windows were up, and the rain was beating down hard. It would have been difficult to hear or smell anything under those conditions.

The driver had stopped the car and the creature froze watching them for a few seconds. At that point the driver put the car in reverse and slowly started to back up. The creature took a couple steps toward the car keeping about the same distance away as before.

The driver again stopped the car, and the creature did likewise. After a short time, the driver put the car in low and began creeping toward the creature. The creature stood still and did not move from the spot where it stopped.

It did put its arms forward as if to protect itself. The car continued to move forward very slowly to the point where both occupants could feel the car make contact with the creature. It put its arms out and placed its hands on the front of the car, with the bumper against its legs.

The driver stopped again and did not try to force his way through. The driver said he was ready to shift to reverse again and "get the hell out of there". It was at that point the creature removed its hands from the car, took about one step forward then proceeded to walk into the woods below the road. That was the last it was seen. The witnesses went home, and I was contacted next day via my website reporting form.

I followed up and did a personal interview on 5-11-2016. The above information was obtained at that time. I also examined the car for any evidence of contact. None was found. The car was also checked using UV / IR light for evidence of handprints or skin oils where the creature is alleged to have been in contact.

Nothing was found; however, it must also be noted that they drove home about 7 miles in driving rain. It is possible any residue could have been washed off. I also went to the area on Mud Pike where the creature was seen in an attempt to find any tracks or other evidence however nothing was found. Much gravel and other debris was washed into the road from the heavy rain so I would expect any such evidence, if it existed, was destroyed.

My impression of both witnesses is that they seem credible. I detected no sign they were seeking notoriety or wanted publicity. Both gave the same impression of the event; frightening yet both wanted answers to what they experienced.

No subsequent reports of any other sightings as of this time. If any come in, they will be referenced to this report.

J. Brown, Investigator

Large Footprints in Fresh Snow Suddenly End North Huntingdon, PA
January, 2018

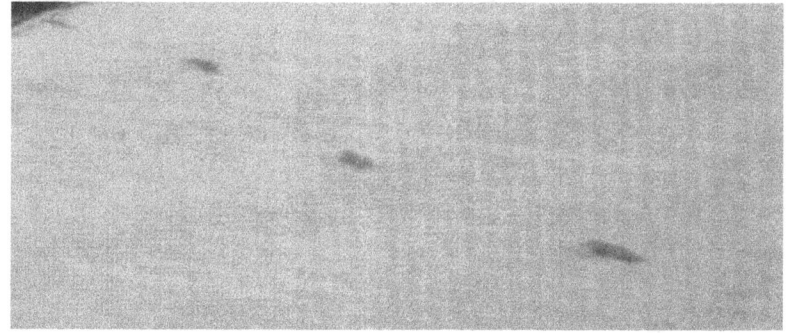

Still capture from video used with permission of the witness.

I have been researching Bigfoot and other phenomena since 1959 and began to conduct in the field investigations in 1965. It was during the major Bigfoot and UFO outbreak that occurred in Pennsylvania in 1973, that some very strange details began to surface concerning these mysterious creatures.

My research teams were responding to these incidents as they were being reported, and we were on the scene of many of these incidents within minutes to hours after they had occurred. We interviewed many frightened witnesses, observed unusual animal reactions that were common with dogs that were close to a Bigfoot, and observed various types of physical evidence at some locations.

Some of the initial occurrences that caught our attention were cases where trails of odd footprints with large strides would be observed over a distance in various ground conditions, then just suddenly stop without explanation. Over the years, this has also been seen in fresh heavy snow. There were no other tracks around and no evidence of a hoax.

There is a comment I recall from one witness from the 1973 Bigfoot wave. The man was a non-believer in Bigfoot until he had one standing only a few feet away from his mobile home. The witness was terrified as he called the state police to report the close encounter with the creature.

The fellow had cut his lawn that evening and the creature left its' fourteen inch-long tracks in the fresh cut grass and on his patio where it was observed. In one area, the tracks ended abruptly. The witness, after seeing that the tracks had just stopped, asked me if these creatures could fly, since what he saw was so unusual.

Bigfoot may not be able to fly, but many reports from people from widespread areas of the state as well as from across the country and elsewhere indicate that there may be more to Bigfoot than just an unknown flesh and blood animal specimen.

In my book, *Silent Invasion: The Pennsylvania UFO-Bigfoot Casebook*, I go into detail of many of the very strange cases of the early 1970's that suggests this possibility. Years ago, I began to question the lack of a body being found after so many years of observations.

I receive reports of Bigfoot sightings, cryptids, and UFOs on a yearly basis from Pennsylvania and elsewhere. Some very strange details continue to be reported with some of these creature encounters. My illustrated lecture, "Strange Aspects of the Elusive Bigfoot", delves deeply into information that suggests that at least some Bigfoot creatures appear to be something other than a mysterious unclassified animal.

I received a video of a series of large footprints in fresh snow that was taken in January of 2018, in North Huntingdon Township,

Pennsylvania. It had snowed during the early morning hours and the family noticed them when they looked outside. I interviewed the wife and husband whose property this had taken place at. They recalled seeing a series of footprints about sixteen inches long with a stride of about four to five feet between each track.

The family was startled because the tracks seemed to just suddenly appear in the yard with no entrance point, then continued on about seventy feet across the yard. The tracks continued until they reached a play area for children and then suddenly just stopped. A witness in this case made a similar comment to the one made by the 1973 witness that I had referred to earlier. "Like something was walking then flew away or something like that." The general area where these tracks were found has a long history of Bigfoot encounters.

Daylight Bigfoot Encounter Reported in Washington County
May 16, 2018

This incident was referred to me by researcher Kevin Paul.

On the afternoon of May 16, 2018, a person was driving their vehicle on a rural road near the border of Washington and Greene counties in Pennsylvania. The driver noticed a truck pulled off to the side of the country road, and the person by the truck and a passenger inside were pointing towards the hillside which was about fifty yards away.

It was then that the first driver noticed something unusual. Stepping out of the tree line was a large upright creature covered with black/brown hair. It was estimated to be at least six and a half to seven feet tall from that distance. The arms were long and hung down by its side. It walked on two legs. At that distance, the witness could not make out any facial features, but stated it had no muzzle, and was certain that it was not a bear.

The creature was observed as it stepped out of the tree line and took four or five steps, then walked back into the tree line and wasn't observed again. The witness heard no unusual sounds and didn't notice any odd smells. The witness was concerned that no one would believe her, however, she was certain that she had seen something unusual.

Family Members Describe Close Range Bigfoot Encounter Near Pittsburgh
July 14, 2018

This sketch by Dave Dragosin was based on the interview with the eyewitness.

A member of a family contacted me concerning an incident that had taken place on July 14, 2018, at a family picnic in a rural location outside of Pittsburgh. The person that I initially interviewed by phone sounded very sincere and provided a detailed account of a strange encounter that he as well as various relatives experienced who attended the event that day. During the extended conversation, I was also able to interview some other family members who told me about what had occurred. They sounded shaken as they described the encounter that had taken place.

One witness I spoke with saw a creature at close range that was similar to other Bigfoot reports that I was aware of from around the Pittsburgh area. I was able to obtain a lot of information from those involved concerning the unusual experiences that had occurred.

The family members, who didn't want to be identified, were perplexed over what had taken place and were looking for answers to what had occurred. I contacted two experienced Bigfoot Investigators, Dave and Cindy Dragosin who lived in the Pittsburgh area as well. The Dragosins, while independent investigators, also collaborate with other Bigfoot research groups such as the Keystone Bigfoot Project, Pennsylvania Cryptozoological Society, and Goosebumps Paranormal. Dave has become well known as a Bigfoot eyewitness forensic artist, where he sketches the creatures described by witnesses whom he has interviewed.

Dave and Cindy arranged to meet with family members during daylight at the location where the encounter had taken place. The witnesses were reluctant to return to that location after dark. The investigators interviewed those involved, took pictures, and gathered other information, and Dave sketched the creature based on the testimony of an eyewitness.

The following details were obtained from the investigation report by Dave and Cindy Dragosin. Some information was edited to protect the confidentiality of those involved.

> On Sunday, July 14, 2018, nine family members along with their large dog began their day-long family picnic during the late afternoon. They were planning to dance, play music, and cook a lot of food and meat on the grill to celebrate a birthday. The children were running around in the woods gathering dead tree limbs to be used for fuel in the campfire for later that evening. There was no electricity in the area, and they had to use the water source available nearby.
>
> The tantalizing aroma of the food and meat cooking filled the surrounding wooded area. Shortly after 11p.m., many of the

personal belongings and picnic items began to be placed in the family cars, but the campfire remained lit and the karaoke machine kept on playing, with the family dancing and singing around the campfire.

At approximately 11:30 that evening, the family dog became agitated by something moving rather stealthily in the woods just to the east of a nearby structure. This very large dog began to growl and bark in a rather agitated manner. Whatever was moving from east to south in the perimeter surrounding the structure began to growl back at the canine.

This commotion caused a male adult, who was standing approximately 15 to 20 yards away, to draw his attention toward the location where the water was located, and the wooded area south of the structure. As the growling continued, growing louder with more intensity, the man noticed a form emerging from the shadows of the trees into the light of the campfire and before his eyes he observed a very, very big, hairy humanoid like creature.

The witness was mesmerized for a brief moment as the creature stood with legs apart and its long arms outstretched exuding intimidation. The man estimated that the creature stood around 8 feet tall. The creature appeared to be very muscular and massive with broad shoulders and covered with long dark hair.

The witness stated that he could hear the creature breathing profoundly and heavily, as he watched its huge chest moving in and out. The man was immediately struck with fear because not only of the creature's size but also said this huge hominid like creature had glowing red eyes. The witness for about 10-15 seconds was able to see the full-frontal appearance of the creature, but it was too dark to see any facial characteristics or other specific details.

The man also recalled there was a brief moment where the creature was swaying back and forth, from left to right for only a couple of times. Then in an instant, the creature turned to its right and ran extremely fast toward the same direction from which it came into the northeast woods. Another young boy said that he also saw the creature run back into the woods.

In the meantime, the dog, tethered nearby, continued to bark furiously in what members of the family say was a rather agitated and defensive manner. Two women ran to their cars parked near the structure, turned on the ignition and adjusted the cars so that the car's headlights faced into the woods in anticipation of seeing what was fleeing from their picnic area.

All of the frightened family members said they could feel the ground beneath them resound from the size and weight of the creature, as it fled the vicinity through dark dense wooded area. None of the other family members stated they actually saw a full-frontal version of the creature, only a brief silhouette of its movement through the woods.

Following the experience on July 14th, the children were rounded up, placed in their respective vehicles, all belongings were gathered, and the campfire was extinguished in order to vacate the picnic site as quickly as possible.

During a one-on-one, face to face interview session that was set up with the family, it was noted that all family members were quite sincere in their reiteration of the event. It was determined that what they saw was a true to life changing encounter. Each and every one of the family adult members were anxious to interpret what they were able to hear, and that was the vocalizations between their pet dog and the creature growling, snarling, and chortling at each other. The temperature that evening was very humid, in the mid-70s, and the skies were clear. Other than growls and snarls, there were no other external vocalizations or odors emitted from the creature.

It was also noted and agreed upon that just prior to the creature's appearance, the aroma of cooked meat and various food lingered, along with the children and women shouting, laughing, and playing gleefully around the campfire and songs were being sung in preparation of singing Happy Birthday and cutting the cake. Unfortunately, that part of the birthday celebration never happened that night.

When the investigators returned to the site at a later date and the exact location was pointed out to the investigators, the tree that the creature stood by was measured and the head of the creature was approximately at an 11-foot mark on the tree.

Excerpt from Dave and Cindy Dragosins report.

Addendum: Historically, there have been numerous reports of Bigfoot encounters originating from throughout the greater Pittsburgh area and surrounding counties. These incidents continue to be reported yearly from throughout the state. The creature may have been attracted to this location by the smell of the food cooking and by the human activity that was taking place.

There have been numerous incidents reported where these large hair covered creatures have thrown large rocks and tree limbs in the direction of humans that were nearby. This has suggested to some researchers that they are marking their territory and want the trespassers to leave.

As in this case, the creatures have at times approached within close range of the observers but generally move off from the area once they are seen. This creature seemed curious of the human activities but did not approach any further into the picnic area to harm the individuals.

Another interesting detail: Within the same hour that this Bigfoot incident took place, a UFO sighting had been reported only miles away hovering over a suburb of Pittsburgh.

Possible Bigfoot Activity Ongoing in Pennsylvania During 2018

Odd tree damage.

In January 2018, large tracks were seen in the snow in Fayette County. In February, odd tracks were also reported in the snow in Armstrong County. Since May, there have been ongoing reports coming in from widespread locations of unusual sounds being reported from wooded areas. Some of the people who have heard these vocalizations are experienced outdoorsmen or hunters and are quite familiar with the area wildlife noises. They are baffled by what they and their neighbors have been hearing.

There have been reports of horrible screams that have massive volume, of monkey sounds, and of various other odd calls reported from various areas from the southwest section of the state. Local residents are independently reporting not only the odd vocalizations, but also the sounds of breaking and falling trees, and in some cases, the sound of what seems to be heavy bipedal footsteps. At some locations, animals seem frightened, and the local nature sounds suddenly just stop when these loud vocalizations are heard.

In August, Eric Altman, Director of the Pennsylvania Cryptozoology Society, and I were investigating recent incidents deep in the woods at locations of Westmoreland and Armstrong counties, where residents had been reporting these activities. In Armstrong County some interesting tree damage was found on healthy trees, where limbs appeared twisted about nine to ten feet off the ground.

At a heavily wooded location in Westmoreland County where there has been a history of Bigfoot activity around the general area, a flattened area about eight feet long, was discovered by the property owner. This did not look like a deer bedding area or related to weather damage that I have seen many times over the years. It looked as though some large animal may have been lying in that location. There is no way to say it was Bigfoot, but similar flattened areas have been seen over the years at locations where we had investigated possible Bigfoot activity.

When I lectured in this part of the state several people approached me, some very privately, and shared their personal accounts of seeing what they believed was a Bigfoot. Some folks brought interesting photos of footprints to share that they had found at various locations. Some people had talked with friends or relatives who had had recent encounters. Some of them shared these incidents but told me the witnesses were reluctant to come forward fearing that they wouldn't be believed.

Stan looking at a flattened area in rural Westmoreland County, PA, where possibly a large animal had been lying down.

I have received a report from a rural location outside of West Newton, that a series of strange whoop calls were heard, and later the sound of three heavy footsteps were also heard in the area where the whoop sounds were coming from. This area has had a history of Bigfoot sightings since the late 1960s.

CREEPY CRYPTIDS

Bigfoot-Like Creature Observed Twenty feet Away on the Derry Side of the Chestnut Ridge
October 1, 2018

A woman was taking a walk in a wooded location on the Derry, PA, side of the Chestnut Ridge. It was just before noon on October 1, 2018, as she was approaching a tree line when she began to hear a series of what sounded like loud knocks on trees that seemed to be originating nearby. The witness recalled that when she heard the knocks, she began to have a strong feeling of fear. The woman was not usually fearful when walking in the woods.

She looked into the woods and noticed a dark tree trunk and also a black shadow. Her first thought was that it was a bear, which are not uncommon in the area. Whatever it was, it didn't move at that time. She looked down toward the ground then up again when a few more knocks occurred. She felt at that point that something was very close by and was trying to scare her into leaving the area.

As the woman focused on the tree trunk about twenty feet away, she realized that there was a large dark humanoid creature hugging the tree as though trying to camouflage itself. The creature was about seven feet tall and was covered with black hair that looked to be about three inches in length. The creature seemed to be tall and thin, but she couldn't see the shoulders or lower extremities clearly due to the way the creature was positioned against the tree.

She could see that the face looked pale and wasn't sure if there was any hair on it. The nose wasn't prominent and seemed to be pushed in. There was no muzzle like a bear. The witness could not see any ears on the creature. The physical feature that caught her attention were the eyes of the creature. The eyes were larger than that of a human and more rounded. The eyes were very dark or black in color. The creature was shifting its eyes around nervously, moving them back and forth. When the eyes were shifted in a corner, she could see white around them. The witness commented that it had "alien looking eyes."

The creature had both of its very long hairy arms wrapped around the trunk of the tree. The hair on the arms was black and wiry. The creature had its cheek against the tree, and it was looking in her direction. It gave the impression that it was trying to hide from the witness.

The woman stated that she was "way too close" to this thing and felt very frightened and ran to a tree about ten feet away. She stood behind the tree and hid. She waited there while she got enough courage to go back and try to get a picture of the creature with her phone on her camera.

She hurriedly went back to the location where she saw the creature and began to snap some pictures of the area. But she did not see the creature again. She stood there for a few minutes when two deer approached from her left. She watched the deer as they moved away. The woman took some pictures of the deer then left the area. She wasn't that far away from where the creature had been, and never heard any sound of it moving out of the area.

The witness told me that she felt as though she had surprised the creature and that it didn't want to be seen which is why it was trying to blend in with the tree. The expression on its face was not one of anger, but that it might have been scared realizing that the witness could see it.

The woman stated that the fear she felt while in the presence of the creature "was more fear than it should have been for a bear." The witness had never seen anything like this before and said she was shocked when she saw it.

Addendum: This was the second close encounter with a Bigfoot-like cryptid reported from Derry Township within a month.

CREEPY CRYPTIDS

The area around Derry Township in Westmoreland County, PA along the Chestnut Ridge has historically been one of the most active locations in the country for Bigfoot sightings and encounters with other cryptids, UFOs, and various other phenomena. Strange encounters are reportedly yearly from this general area.

Motorist Five Feet From Bigfoot on a Country Road November 9, 2018

On the evening of November 9, 2018, I received a phone call from motorist who sounded quite shook up and described to me in great detail an encounter he had just had with a very strange creature about fifteen minutes earlier.

The man was driving alone on a dark country road in the region known as the Mon Valley outside of Pittsburgh. It was a cold and rainy evening. As he drove down the road, he noticed four or five deer running down the bank ahead of him as though alarmed by something. He continued down the road for a short distance. The driver had his headlights on low as he approached a straight stretch of road. About fifty feet away, he noticed something standing on the left side of the roadway.

He slowly moved closer to that area and put on his high beams since he was unsure as to what he was seeing. Suddenly, a huge hair covered creature walked out onto the roadway about five feet in front of his vehicle. The witness was stunned as the creature stopped on the road and turned and looked directly at him. The creature then turned and ran off taking very long strides as it leaped across the road from left to right. The witness could see its long arms swinging as it ran. The hands of the creature were in a closed or, as the witness stated, "in a cuffed position".

The creature continued to run up a slight hill. The motorist told me he grabbed for his cell phone to try to take a picture and followed the creature in his vehicle for a very short distance. He was right behind it, but suddenly the huge creature was gone from sight and it seemed to have just vanished.

In a matter of seconds, he lost sight of it and didn't see it again. This sudden disappearance baffled the witness since he felt that he should have been able to see where the creature had moved to. There is the possibility that the creature could have moved off to the side and outside of the illumination range from the headlights. The witness was sure of what he saw.

The witness called a relative immediately after the incident and told him what had occurred. That person looked up my phone number and told him to call me. The witness told me about what had occurred and stated to me, "I have chills right now. It scared me so bad". I was able to conduct an interview with the driver and he was able to provide a detailed account of what he saw and what had taken place.

The creature, he said, stood at least seven feet tall. It was covered with shaggy brown and black hair on much of the body. The witness stated, however, the creature looked unhealthy as though it was sick. There were areas on the body where the hair was missing or sparse as though it might have mange.

The head was the size of a watermelon and somewhat peanut shaped. The face was long and narrow. The ears could not be seen due to the hair in that area. The nose appeared large and about four inches long. The cheeks were sunk in and looked unhealthy.

The driver said he could not see the mouth due to the hair cover. The chest had a sparse amount of hair compared to the creature's back that was covered in hair. The arms were long and hang down to at least the kneecaps. The hands were about twice the size of an adult human. They were brown in color and hairy.

The lower leg section could not be seen when it stood close to the car since it was blocked from view. The witness told me that the creature looked very muscular and that the shoulders were massive. The waist was thinner.

It was the eyes of the creature that was most frightening to the observer. The eyes were larger than that of a human and they were luminous. The man stated that they were "beet red." The luminosity was described as shiny "like flashlights". The driver said the creature looked directly at him eye to eye then turned and ran off. The entire encounter lasted for just several seconds. No unusual odors or sounds were noticed during the encounter.

The witness had always been skeptical of the existence of Bigfoot. He confessed that he had never been so scared in his life, particularly when the creature looked directly into his eyes. He told me that there is no possible way that this could have been a person in a costume from its massive size and how fast it moved.

Addendum: I spoke with a relative of the driver a short time after our interview on the night of the encounter. He told me that the witness was very frightened.

The next day, Eric Altman, Director of the Pennsylvania Cryptozoological Society, and I went to the location of the Bigfoot encounter to meet with the witness and search for evidence.

There had been a lot of rain overnight and the area was covered in leaves so no tracks were found. Near the side of the road where the creature was first seen standing, we did find an area of foliage that was flattened as well as a single branch in a tree was broken in half about seven feet off the ground.

The witness, who appeared to still be shaken over the experience, was able to show us the exact area where the creature stood and moved, and he reenacted the movements of the creature. The witness was very sincere and credible and quite believable.

Addendum 2: This general area in the Mon Valley has had a long history of Bigfoot encounters going back to at least the early 1970s. I investigated many creature encounters in this area over the years as well as in more recent times. Bigfoot encounters continued to be reported in Pennsylvania in 2018 from around the greater Pittsburgh area and other parts of the state.

Bigfoot Vanishes on Toll Road Near Delmont November 28, 2018

I received a phone call from a man who was driving on Toll Road 66 toward Delmont, on the evening of November 28, 2018. He had a strange incident take place that he wanted to relate to me.

It was around 9:30 PM, there was some fog in the area at the time. About two hundred feet ahead in the middle of the highway, he noticed something tall that was just standing there. As he approached closer, in his headlights he saw the gray shadowy silhouette of a tall upright creature that he estimated was seven to eight feet tall. He slowed his vehicle down.

The creature had broad shoulders and long arms and legs. He was not able to make out any facial features. He only saw it for about ten to twenty seconds. Then the experience got stranger. The witness said the creature never walked off the highway- it just suddenly vanished.

Another car pulled up next to his vehicle and that driver put his window down. He yelled to the witness, "Did you see that?" Both drivers left the area perplexed as to what had just happened.

CREEPY CRYPTIDS

Strange Trail of Footprints Observed in the Snow in Derry Township
January 21, 2019

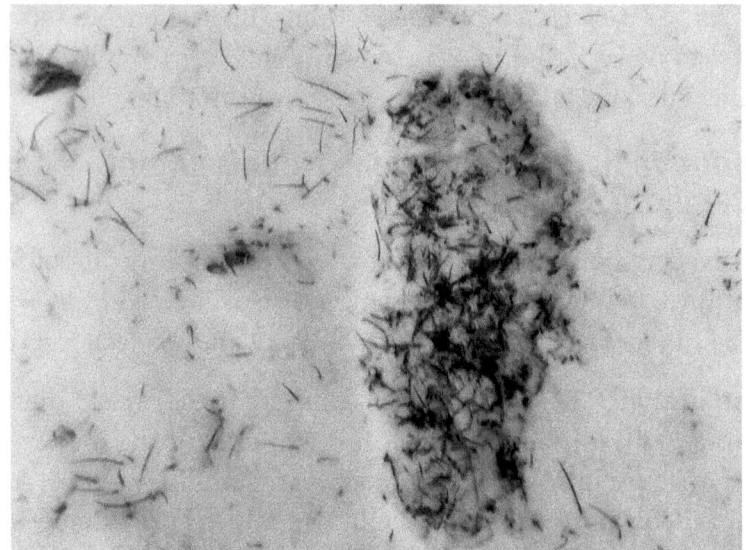

Photo used with permission of the witness.

On the morning of January 21, 2019, a resident in Derry Township, Westmoreland County, noticed a series of unusual footprints in the snow. The witness observed numerous tracks that moved down a hill and continued into the distance. The tracks were estimated to be about eight to ten inches in length and about seven inches wide at the toes.

These tracks are smaller than some of the other footprints that have been found in this general area. Very similar tracks that are similar in size and configuration have been found in past years along the Loyalhanna Creek as well the Derry area and in the vicinity of the Chestnut Ridge.

The Chestnut Ridge is known for its long history of strange encounters with UFOs, Bigfoot, cryptids, as well as many other anomalies. For many years, Bigfoot tracks and other unusual footprints have shown up on the ridge and in nearby locations.

Bigfoot Encounter Was Like Watching a Predator Movie
February 9, 2019

*Drawing of a Bigfoot,
used with permission of Forensic Bigfoot Artist Dave Dragosin.*

CREEPY CRYPTIDS

A husband and wife were on their way to work during the early morning hours in February of 2019. It was still dark outside, and the driver was watching ahead in the distance for any deer. They were driving on a rural road a few miles outside of Greensburg. His wife was able to provide a detailed account of the creature that was observed about fifty feet ahead of them.

On the side of the road and then walking into a wooded section of woods was a tall hair covered man-like creature. According to the woman, what was observed could have only been a Bigfoot. The height of the beast was estimated to be approximately seven and one half to eight feet tall. It was covered with dark brown hair. The head appeared to be large and seemed to sit directly on its shoulders as there was no apparent neck. The creature, which had very broad shoulders, looked massive and walked somewhat stooped.

At the angle the creature was observed, facial features could not be seen. However, the cheek area seemed lighter than the surrounding hair. There did not appear to be any facial hair. The large hands of the animal were bent and curved and looked like they were cupped under. The arms were very long and did not appear to swing when it moved. When I interviewed the wife, she stated that while the observation was quick, she was able to get a good view of the strange creature from head to toe.

But she was baffled by how that huge creature seemed to suddenly just appear then vanish. "He was all of a sudden there out of nowhere and then disappeared." She stated that it was like watching the original Predator movie where the alien creature becomes visible and invisible at times. "I feel like he was gone before I could blink or even look away."

Addendum: As I mentioned elsewhere in this book and in my other writings, there are other similar encounters in Pennsylvania and around the country where in some Bigfoot cases the creatures seem to be able to appear and disappear.

The Small Bigfoot and the Strange Light
May 2019

A strange incident was reported from a rural area of Allegheny County not far from Pittsburgh at about 1 AM in early May of 2019. A man was looking out of his back window of his home when he saw something unusual that caught his attention. The witness observed a creature that stood between four and one half to five feet tall that was covered with dark hair, with longer hair in the head and back area.

The creature was walking on two legs and the arms extended almost down to the knees. The man could see that the arms were swinging. The area was illuminated by some outdoor lighting which provided a good view to the observer.

The creature moved fast with a long stride and was observed at a distance of approximately seventy five feet. The creature had crossed a fence into a neighbor's yard and then entered a wooded area about one hundred feet away and was no longer observed.

About three seconds later at the same position where the creature had entered into the woods, a bright sphere of light about three to four inches in diameter suddenly appeared. The witness said it was similar to looking directly into the front of a flashlight and it was about four feet above the ground.

The light then moved a short distance for about three seconds and vanished. About four to five seconds, later the light appeared again about ten feet away. This time the small sphere emitted a bright beam of light in that area. The beam extended out to about ten to twelve feet. The beam was observed for a few seconds before it vanished and was not seen again.

Creepy Cryptids

Stan Gordon

Chapter Four

Thunderbird Sightings

Reported sightings of huge, over-sized birds and other enormous and very strange flying creatures have been ongoing for many years across the country as well as in the Keystone state. There is no doubt that some observations were misidentifications of some of the native bird species common to Pennsylvania. Most commonly would have been observations of turkey vultures, eagles, and the great blue herons. Some thunderbird sightings had taken place near wetlands and lake areas where some of these species would frequent.

It is very difficult for a witness to give a good estimate in altitude and size concerning a UFO or a thunderbird sighting. However, there have been many observations of both anomalies when they were seen at very low altitude, close to the ground (or in some cases on the ground) and quite close to the onlooker.

I began to investigate reports of these giant flying monstrosities after I started my in the field investigations of various phenomena that the public was reporting during the later 1960s. Many of the thunderbird encounters that I have investigated describe a huge bird similar to a well over-sized turkey vulture that was generally dark brown or black in color.

CREEPY CRYPTIDS

There are, however, numerous reports of massive flying creatures that are considerably more unusual.

- There are also reports of massive featherless flying creatures covered with a leathery skin over the bones. Some witnesses described these creatures as looking like giant bats. These flying leathery giants were commonly reported to be black or of a darker color.

- Some observers have reluctantly described to me their encounters with huge flying behemoths that they felt looked prehistoric. Some witnesses have provided detailed accounts and physical descriptions of seeing what they believed was a pterodactyl or teratorn.

- Even stranger are accounts of tall winged leathery skinned humanoid beings such as what has become known as the "Butler Gargoyle encounter" that took place in March of 2011 between Chicora and East Brady in Butler County, Pennsylvania. The creature was reportedly seen by a number of other witnesses around that same time period.

- We can't forget the Mothman encounters that took place in neighboring West Virginia during 1966-1967. Many witnesses in the area around Point Pleasant, West Virginia, reported seeing a very tall humanoid creature with wings and luminous red glowing eyes. During 1966, I was hearing rumors that a mysterious creature similar to Mothman, was also making appearances in a rural location outside of the Pittsburgh area.

Since then, I have learned more details. There were reportedly two separate locations where a strange frightening creature was seen and some strange goings on had taken place in Allegheny County during that time period.

The witnesses to these various strange winged creatures- once again- come from all walks of life. Very few observers have any interest in being identified and many feared that they would be laughed at. I have spoken with outdoorsmen, hunters and even experienced bird watchers who have seen some of these odd airborne creatures and who remain baffled by what they saw. Some witnesses told me that what they saw should not exist.

As with other cryptids such as Bigfoot, not all sightings of Thunderbirds or these other strange flying oddities take place in rural or more isolated locations. Many of these encounters have occurred in more populated areas such as over towns and busy highways. I have spoken with a witness who swears to have observed what looked like a pterodactyl over the Freeport bridge years ago.

One location that over the years has had a history of sightings of Thunderbirds has been around the Borough of South Greensburg, Pennsylvania. In the 1990s, a motorist in that area had to suddenly hit his brakes since the road ahead was being blocked by a giant furry black bird that looked something like a vulture. The witness was amazed to see that the wingspan of the huge fowl took up the width of both sides of the roadway. The creature soon flapped its wings and rose into the sky and was gone.

There were also giant bird sightings from areas just miles away near Greensburg, Jeannette, and Derry for example.

Giant Dark Bird Observed in Sewickley Township 2014

The man who reported this incident rarely discussed what took place fearing he wouldn't be believed. This encounter occurred one afternoon and was believed to have been during 2014. The witness was driving on General Braddock Road in Sewickley Township in Westmoreland County.

CREEPY CRYPTIDS

His attention was drawn to a huge bird that banked from the left through the tree line. The giant bird was very low and passed under the trees and was only about thirty feet off the ground. The man watched as creature came out of the tree line and banked to the right and flew out of sight.

He only saw it for seconds, but it was long enough for him to realize that what he saw was unusual. He described the huge flying creature as completely dark brown or black in color. The witness saw the huge bird from its back end. He estimated the body to be about eighteen inches wide. What amazed the witness was the wingspan of the creature that he estimated to be about twelve to fourteen feet wide.

The giant flying creature appeared to just glide across the sky and did not actually flap its huge wings as it moved about twenty five to thirty yards ahead of the witness. The man told me that he couldn't believe what he was seeing. He still thinks about that day and was glad to learn that he wasn't the only person in the area to report seeing something similar in past years.

Huge Bird Swoops Down in Front of Car
July 2017

It was about 10:30 PM on the evening of July 15, 2017. Two people were riding on Mill Road near Big Run, Pa, in Jefferson County. The high beams were on at the time as they drove down the dark road. About ten to twelve feet ahead of the car, they noticed an adult deer was standing on the right side of the road.

Seconds later, a giant bird swooped down from the sky about ten feet away that moved left to right. They could easily see it in the high beams of the headlights. The wings were down when they saw it. They never saw it flap its wings. The entire bird was either dark brown or black in color.

The wingspan of the huge bird appeared to be much larger than the deer. One witness estimated that it easily had ten to twelve foot wingspan. They could see the feathers on it. They could see its long body, very large wingspan, and the head appeared to be flatter, and it was short, and beak was short. They heard no sound. When the bird swooped down it glided two to three feet above the road. It was unsure if the bird was swooping down for the deer.

The total observation was five to six seconds. The other passenger stated, "They had never seen a bird that big before." It looked like it had a head similar to an eagle, but the head was flatter and had a short beak.

Thunderbird Sightings Near the Chestnut Ridge? January 2018

Up on the Chestnut Ridge not far from Ligonier, people are again seeing huge birds at close range and on the ground. One witness said some of these huge flying creatures that were "big and black" had wing spans that were estimated to be around twenty feet wide. This area has had a history of giant birds with massive wingspans that have been reported for years. The people who have seen them are all familiar with the large birds in the area such as turkey vultures and blue herons and are sure these are something quite different.

CREEPY CRYPTIDS

A section of the Chestnut Ridge near Derry, PA, where many Bigfoot and other cryptid encounters have been reported for many years.

Huge Bird With Strange Tail Observed Near Belle Vernon January 25, 2019

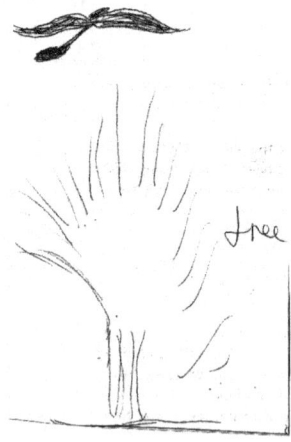

Drawing used with permission of the witness.

On the afternoon of January 25, 2019, a family went shopping in the Belle Vernon area. The witnesses were parked in a car when they noticed something that looked unusual in the sky. They observed a very large dark bird with an extensive wingspan flying over some trees. It was moving about fifty to sixty feet above the ground.

It had its small head tucked under and the feet could not be seen. The physical feature that caught their attention was its unusual tail. At the end of the tail was what appeared to be a football shaped appendage. It was unlike any current bird species that they were familiar with.

Another Possible Thunderbird Sighting in the Mon Valley July 2020

A man was outside one evening in July of 2020 when his attention was drawn to the sky over the Monongahela River near Monessen, Pennsylvania. It was about dusk and there was still a lot of light from the orange hue in the sky. The witness had a nice scenic view of the area from where he was located.

What caught his eye was a large black object in the sky moving north toward the river. The witness at first thought that it was an aircraft. That was until he saw that the wings were flapping very slowly. The wings were narrow and had a slight arc to them. The bird had to be huge to be so large from the distance he was from it.

The man watched the giant winged creature for a few minutes as it moved from left to right with very slow flaps of its wings. It appeared to mainly glide through the sky while it was observed. The man was able to watch it also with binoculars until it moved out of sight. The witness was familiar with the birds in the area and was certain this was something much more unusual. He felt that this creature was some type of scavenger.

CREEPY CRYPTIDS

Stan Gordon

Chapter Five

What Mysterious Beasts Lurk Below the Water?

There have been reports of mysterious creatures observed in the swamps, rivers, and lakes across Pennsylvania.

Mysterious aquatic creatures have reportedly been seen in the lakes and rivers of Pennsylvania for many years. During the early 1970s, talk radio was becoming popular in the Pittsburgh area. I was frequently being invited as a guest to discuss UFOs and cryptids on these live interview shows.

I recall on various occasions that callers would tell me about seeing what they described as giant snakes or huge serpent-like creatures swimming in the Monongahela and Ohio rivers around Pittsburgh. I have spoken with people who lived along the Mon and recall stories from locals going back to the 1940s who claimed to have seen something very large in the water they could not identify.

In March of 2008, near Loch 3 near Pittsburgh, a witness swore that he saw a twenty foot long snake-like creature with huge eyes that had a yellow ring around a black pupil. In the mouth of the giant serpent was either a deer or a large dog that it dragged under the water. There have been other accounts since then from areas along the Monongahela River area.

There have been reports from Kinzua Lake in Warren County of a creature that I was told was nicknamed, "The Kinzua Dragon" by some of the locals. Over the years, there have been sightings and photographs taken of the mysterious water beast that supposedly prowls the waters of Raystown Lake in Huntingdon County. That creature has become known as "Raystown Ray."

I spoke with another witness who, in about 2015, observed something at another lake park in Westmoreland County. Something like a huge eel with luminous red eyes reportedly stood up in the water and then moved toward the shore.

One of the best-known bizarre water beasts is "Bessie" that has reportedly been seen in the waters of Lake Erie. I interviewed a witness who claims to have actually seen the creature out of the water and resting on a section of Presque Isle Beach around the mid 1990s.

The creature he saw was estimated to be over forty feet long, with skin texture similar to an elephant. It had flippers like a sea turtle, however, its tail was blocked by the high grass in the area. He felt that what he saw should not have been in existence. It looked like a prehistoric creature known as a plesiosaur.

I also interviewed witnesses who saw something very long and dark swimming near some docks at a fishing spot in Fayette County in 2019. The long black submerged water creature appeared to have a domed shape front. Whatever the creature was, it swam out toward the deeper part of the water.

One fellow went to obtain a spotlight to try to see the creature, but it was not seen again. Those who saw it are very familiar with the larger fish in the area and this was something they could not identify. They had heard stories that other people in past years had watched a large strange aquatic animal in the same area.

I had heard these stories of strange water monsters for many years. In my earlier days I used to fish in various streams in the state. I saw some very large catfish and carp. I have felt that some of these reports were likely some over-sized fish that people have misidentified. But when considering the reports, many other credible people have also provided me detailed accounts of seeing some water creatures that are indeed strange and not something common to the locations where they were seen.

Two Fisherman Watch Strange Creature Rise From the Monongahela River Near Pittsburgh
1980s

A very nice individual was kind enough to share this account with me. It was during the late 1980s when two fellows were doing some early morning fishing caught sight of something quite strange. They were fishing on the Monongahela River near Pittsburgh. They had been fishing at that spot for several hours but didn't have any bites.

They were packing up their gear when suddenly, the head of a strange beast came up out of the water about fifteen feet away. Whatever it was, the head was all black in color and was about the size of a soccer ball. The observers also noticed that it had two cats sized ears that came to a point. The eyes were black and piercing.

The creature looked directly at the fisherman. Moments later it dropped back down into the water then resurfaced a second then a third time. The shape of a dark long creature could be seen under the water as it moved off in the distance.

What Was in the River Under the Rankin Bridge? 1980s

Over the years I have continued to hear stories about strange activity that has taken place in the Monongahela River and other rivers around Pittsburgh. A witness told me that he was taking a break from his job and was outside enjoying the weather in the summer during the 1980s.

It was still light outside but dusk was approaching. He had a good view of the river from his location. Suddenly, he noticed something unusual that was occurring in the river underneath the Rankin Bridge. The witness estimated that he was less than a quarter mile away from that area. What he saw he couldn't really understand.

There was a disturbance in the river, and something large suddenly rose up and broke the water surface. It then went back down into the river and once again rose up out of the water and went back down again and was not seen after that. The witness didn't know if it was some type of living creature or something else. It sure has made him wonder over the years.

It Rose From the Swamp in Fayette County 2016

I first met these witnesses at an Outdoor EXPO in 2019. I later conducted a follow up interview with the two men concerning the following incident.

Stan Gordon

It was on a warm evening in 2016 when the two men went fishing in a swampy area of Fayette County. The men had been there a while when the one fellow realized that his fishing line had become lodged in the water. They decided it was time to leave so they started to pack up their gear and the one man took the equipment back to the truck.

The other fisherman stayed behind trying to dislodge the hook instead of having to cut the fishing line. The man heard a commotion in the water. About ten to twelve feet away, the man was startled when a large creature suddenly rose straight up out of the water.

It was getting dark, but what the witness saw looked like a tall humanoid-like being. It was of a dark color and appeared to be covered with fur. There was water dripping off the body. The general shape appeared to be relatively thin and over six feet tall. The man estimated that the creature weighed about one hundred ninety pounds. The arms and legs were not clearly seen during the short observation.

As the creature rose from the water it turned its head and looked directly at the started observer. The feature that the man remembers clearly was the odd-looking eyes of the beast. The eyes were catlike with a black slit through the center. The eyes were luminous and glowing bright yellow.

The witness also told me that it was very strange how this strange animal suddenly just rose up out of the water as though it was somewhat like a large reptile with its movement. The frightened man immediately grabbed the rest of his gear and ran back to the truck telling the other fellow to get out of here.

CREEPY CRYPTIDS

A Massive Disturbance in the Monongahela River Early July 2020

I received this report from a person who had spent much of their life boating and fishing on the Monongahela River. The witness contacted me because of an unusual occurrence that had taken place during the afternoon in early July of 2020. It was a nice day, and few people were around at the time.

There were two people involved who were fishing on the Monongahela River not far from Nemacolin in Greene County. They were trolling at the time when one witness looked toward the back of the boat. As that person looked at the fishing line, a massive force of water rose up from the river just behind the boat, spraying water into the air. It rose up to about three feet and created a forty to fifty foot circle on the surface and then went back down under the river.

What was in the water that created this huge water surge was not discernible. Both people aboard the boat observed this occurrence. The witness I talked with was terrified by what took place and was very concerned over this very powerful force that made no sound at the time that this occurred.

Addendum: This report seems to have some similarities to the previous case that was reported to have taken place in the 1980s on the Mon River under the Rankin Bridge.

There have been rumors for many years and even legends dating back to the Native Americans of a strange water monster that was said to live in the depths of the Mon River. Maybe there is some truth to some of these stories.

Stan Gordon

Chapter Six

Those Mysterious Black Panthers

Black jaguars or leopards are commonly referred to as black panthers. These animals are not supposed to exist in Pennsylvania, but the sightings continue.

There are two categories of mystery large felines that have commonly been reported for many years across Pennsylvania, namely mountain lions and black panthers.

CREEPY CRYPTIDS

Mountain Lions

The mountain lion, also known as a cougar or puma, commonly prowled the forests of the Keystone state. However, in the late 1800's, it is said the last native mountain lion had been shot. These animals were thought to have been extirpated and no longer lurking in our woodlands.

I made this cast of what is believed to be the paw print of a mountain lion. It was taken on July 25, 1984, in South Buffalo Township, in Armstrong County.

The sightings of these animals, however, have never ceased, and these reports continue to occur in large numbers. Many credible witnesses claim to have seen these animals and many encounters were in daylight.

During the many years that I investigated these incidents, I heard accounts of more than one adult cougar accompanying another one at the same time, as well as reports of an adult mountain lion with cubs.

Stan Gordon

There have been photos and videos taken of what looks to be a cougar. Many tracks have also been reported and in some cases, casts have been made.

In July of 1984, I was contacted by police in Armstrong County to send up a team to investigate a series of mountain lion sightings that had been reported by the public. During the field research we conducted, a series of paw prints was discovered, and a cast was made of one of the clearer tracks.

For many years, local residents around Armstrong County have been reporting sightings of mountain lions in that area. Such sightings, however, have commonly taken place in southwestern Pennsylvania and throughout many other areas of the state as well.

I have investigated many of these reports over the years and I agree with the game commission that some of these observations were misidentifications of other animals known to roam in these areas.

I had also heard stories years ago that some people had these animals as exotic pets and supposedly released them into the woods when they could no longer control them. There have apparently been some hoax cases as well. Many of the witnesses that I have interviewed including hunters and outdoorsmen are certain that they saw a mountain lion.

Black Panthers

Considerably much stranger are the numerous reports from throughout the state of an animal that witnesses commonly describe as a black panther. They are, of course, referring to the animal that they have often seen caged in zoos across the country such as leopards and jaguars that exist in other parts of the world.

Creatures such as black panthers that are showing up in some parts of the United States and other countries where they should not be lurking have also shown similar characteristics to some of the strange elements that I have found associated with Bigfoot.

In one incident in Fayette County, (where many very strange cases have been reported) a man watched as a black cat physically grew in size until it looked like a black panther that one would see in a zoo.

The creature walked up the road and growled at the man and stared at him with its luminous yellow eyes. He fired his pistol at it but was not sure if he had hit it. The animal suddenly just vanished in front of the startled witness, and it was not seen again. The man's large dog was in a nearby pen but refused to come out after the encounter. Black panthers often show up in areas where Bigfoot is being reported.

The following are some of the fascinating black panther encounters that have come to my attention.

Black Panther Approaches Child on a Camping Adventure 1975

It was in 2019 that I met an individual who shared a personal experience with me concerning a strange encounter that he had as a youngster. It was an experience that he will never forget. The following is a statement that the witness provided to me concerning his close encounter with a creature that he is certain was a black panther. Such an animal is not supposed to be prowling the woods of Pennsylvania.

"The year was about 1975, and I was about four to five years old. My mother, father, and I had gone to visit my mother's side of the family, which resided in the Blairsville area of Indiana County. My mother's younger sister and her husband were very outdoorsy type people and suggested that we go to camping spot that they frequented. We arrived in two vehicles to what was nothing more than a pull off on a dirt road along a power line with a fire pit in the middle of it. I recall a long drive up the road leading to it being treacherous and my father complaining that he was going to rip the muffler off of his car.

After arriving, they started a fire in the pit, and we roasted hotdogs on sticks while passing time. They had laid out sleeping bags, and as the sun went down, my mother told me to go lay down. The sleeping bags were about twenty five feet away from the fire pit, between the vehicles and the fire. The four of them sat around the fire pit as I laid down on one of the sleeping bags. I was drifting off to sleep when I was suddenly jolted by the simultaneous sight of a large black panther creeping toward me and the four of them screaming.

The large black cat suddenly broke from a low creeping crawl into a full sprint between the four of them and myself. It ran right past me while leaving out a loud growl. It quickly disappeared over the hillside and I jumped up along with my father to run over to the side of the hill to get a look at it. It jumped across a ravine and proceeded to run up the power line in giant leaps. We were able to watch it run up the other side of the hill for a short time before losing sight of it. It was a very large cat, with jet black hair, a very long tail, and was extremely muscular.

I was very young at the time but remember it very vividly. My mother and father said that the cat was creeping toward me as I was lying on the sleeping bag and had made it to within a few feet of me before they had spotted it and began screaming. My parents were so shaken by the incident, that we immediately left and drove back home to Monroeville. Of the four people with me, my parents are both passed away and my aunt has suffered a severe stroke, but my uncle remembers it well. He told me that the location was a power line along Route 422, between Strongstown and Indiana, in Indiana County."

Addendum: During a follow up interview, I had with the witness, I learned that the incident had taken place around dusk on the day of the encounter. It was comfortable that evening so while the sleeping bags were laid out, the young witness decided to lay on top of his bag since he was warm enough. He was just dozing off when he was startled by the screams of his parents and the other campers.

The boy looked up to see a huge black cat with a long tail that was very low to the ground and creeping only a few feet from him. He said the body of this creature was about twice the size of a large German Shepard dog, and the tail was at least two feet long. He only caught a glimpse of the face for a second since the animal was staring toward the campfire where the other campers were screaming from. He didn't recall any facial features.

He did recall that he could see the muscles in the front section and back end of the creature. The mysterious feline ran between the young boy and the other four observers. As the creature passed them the boy recalled that it let out a loud and deep growl.

The one detail that caught my attention was that this encounter took place along a power line. Once again, the association of these types of reports with nearby energy sources has been very common.

A Black Panther Encounter With Some Unusual Details 1995

This encounter took place during the summer of about 1995. Two young fellows were taking a walk along a wooded area near Route 66 between the towns of Greensburg and Delmont in Westmoreland County. The fellow's attention was suddenly drawn for some unknown reason to look above them into the trees.

That is when they both saw a large cat-like creature that was walking in the trees about twenty feet overhead. The creature had fur that was solid black in color and the body was about four feet long, which didn't include the tail length.

The boys only saw the strange animal for a few seconds, didn't notice any sound. It seemed as though the creature was unaware of their presence. The two boys looked at each other then looked again for the creature but were unable to observe it again.

The boys ran home and told their family members what they had seen, but they were not taken seriously. The fellows believe that they saw a black panther, a creature that should not be roaming the woods in that part of the world.

The one witness who sent me a statement brought up some unusual details concerning the case. They see an out of place animal at close range. Something caused the fellows to look up at the trees above them at the same time even though they heard no sound.

CREEPY CRYPTIDS

The witness doesn't understand how that large animal was able to walk across those trees at the time. The trees were not thick, and he can't understand how it was able to move over the branches between the trees.

That person, on reflecting back to that day, speculated that the environment had somehow adapted to fit the needs of the creature as it moved through the trees. He never saw any physical changes at that time However, it seemed that the trees seemed a lot denser. When they looked away and then looked back to where the animal had been, the trees appeared normal and thinner.

The fellow wonders if, somehow, he had a glance into another reality or dimension, or maybe it was a hologram projection.

Addendum: There have been many sightings of what people believe were black panthers throughout the state. Many of the sightings have occurred in the southwest section of the state. There have been numerous such encounters reported close to where their sighting took place. Some of these black panther reports also have strange elements to them.

A Black Panther Encounter With a Strange Camera Anomaly July 2018

The witness was deep in the woods riding on four wheeler vehicle in July of 2018. This incident took place near the community of White, PA, in Fayette County. It was around 5 PM, and the weather was gray and cloudy. As the fellow went around a curve in the road, a very large cat-like animal suddenly bolted across the road in front of him about thirty feet away.

The witness, who was familiar with the bobcats and other wildlife in the area, was certain that what he saw was not native to Pennsylvania. He was quite certain that what he saw was a black panther. The animal, which he estimated would weight about sixty five pounds, was covered with short shiny black hair. The tail length could not be seen since it was blocked by some high weeds. The beast was very muscular, and he could see muscles bulge in its chest as it ran nearby.

What caught the attention of the man was when the panther looked directly at him. It had eyes that appeared luminous that were bluish green in color. The creature was in view for about fifteen to twenty seconds. The witness hurried over to where the animal had passed looking for any evidence. There he saw some tracks in a mud hole that the creature had walked through.

He immediately grabbed his fully charged phone to take a camera picture. All of the bars on the phone showed it had a complete charge. He aimed at the tracks and tried to take pictures, but the phone would not function, and the bars indicated that it had no charge. The witness could not understand why the phone wouldn't operate. As soon as he returned home, he went to charge the phone and found that it once again was showing a full charge. The man had no explanation for this camera malfunction.

Addendum: During the many years that I have been investigating UFOs as well as Bigfoot and cryptid cases in the state, some very strange details concerning these encounters have come to my attention. Among the odd events reported are numerous instances where witnesses attempted to take pictures of nearby UFOs or even Bigfoot and other strange creatures but the camera would not work.

There are many instances where fully charged and normal functioning cameras or camera-phones either malfunctioned or immediately lost their battery charge when trying to take a picture of one of these anomalies. In some cases, the device worked fine after the anomaly was no longer present.

I recall a story that a police officer told me during the 1980s. He was investigating a Bigfoot sighting about thirty miles outside of Pittsburgh. There were some strange footprints at the location where the incident had taken place. He brought along the camera that was kept in the office to document police investigations. The camera was used often and had been checked out and was in good condition.

The officer aimed his camera at the tracks, but it would not respond. He tried several more times, but the camera was not operational. He had used the camera many times before and never had a problem with it. He took it back to the office after the incident and tried it again. It was working perfectly normal.

Man Encounters Black Panther Ten Feet Away
March, 2020

A man was doing some outdoor chores during the afternoon at a rural location in the Laurel Highlands. The fellow walked into a building that had the door left open.

The man was walking around looking for some equipment when he was suddenly startled by a large dark animal that emerged from the back of the enclosure, and then ran past him only ten feet away. The body of the animal was about three to three and a half feet in length and was jet black in color and very shiny. It was estimated to weigh about fifty to eighty pounds.

The man could hear the animal as it approached him very closely then continued to run through the open door to the outside and into a nearby wooded area. The witness was alarmed by the size of the animal and the fact that he could hear its paws striking the ground, making a sound as though it was making a fast gallop. The witness only observed the creature for several seconds but was certain that the huge cat-like creature he saw was a black panther.

The witness, who was upset after the encounter, immediately reported to a friend what had taken place. I was contacted later that day. The witness and another person searched the area and found what looked like a large paw print in the area where the animal had been observed.

Black Panther Encountered in Daylight; Cambria County May 27, 2020

It was about 8:40 AM on the morning of May 27, 2020, when three passengers in a car had a strange experience. They were driving very slowly down a country road on their way to one of their favorite fishing spots. The road was very bumpy, so they were only traveling about five miles per hour.

The motorist noticed something large and black sitting in the middle of the road about one hundred twenty feet away. The driver yelled to one of the fellows in the back seat asking him, "What is that big black thing in the middle of the road?" He looked ahead and said that he didn't know what it was. They moved ahead about another ten feet. Suddenly, a very large animal that they described as a black panther rose up from a sitting position and looked towards the vehicle.

Once the animal rose from the ground, they could see its humped back, as it swung its head and looked back directly at the observers. It then started running away from them and really picked up speed once it was about thirty feet away. At one point when the creature made a turn, the entire body of the animal was clearly observed.

The witnesses were unable to see any facial details during the five to seven second encounter. The body of the animal was estimated to be between four to five feet in length, with it long curled tail about three feet or more in length. The entire body was "jet black" in color. The panther ran up over a hill in the vicinity of some high-tension power lines and was not seen again.

The witnesses were shaken up over what they had seen but continued on to do some fishing. About an hour later, a number of geese that were walking around about one hundred yards away suddenly became alarmed and started honking and moved away from that area. About a minute later, the fellows heard several very loud and ferocious sounding growls from the nearby woods. They thought that the black panther was back in the area. The man who had been driving earlier yelled to the other two fellows to pack up !the fishing gear and told them, "Let's get out of here!" which they were all glad to do.

The driver of the vehicle was an experienced outdoorsman. The creature he saw was huge and the largest cat he had ever seen. He was familiar with what a mountain lion looked like and said this animal was much larger. I interviewed him about three hours after the encounter. He told me that his heart was still racing from the experience.

The week before when the man was fishing in that same area, he noticed an odd track that was not well defined. It looked to be somewhat oval shaped about six inches long with possibly four toes.

Black Panther Crosses Field in Daylight; Derry Township June 10, 2020

A man was driving near Derry in Westmoreland County on the morning of June 10, 2020. As he rounded a corner, he hit his brakes because he noticed something unusual in a nearby field. He saw what appeared to be a black panther in the field near a barn.

Stan Gordon

He got a good look at it about eighty to one hundred yards away. The animal was all black. There was a small area at the back end of the animal that looked possibly brown but could have been mud where it had been lying. The body of the animal was about four feet long. The tail was the most impressive feature. It was about three feet long and very thick and all black.

The witness watched the animal a short time, then decided to drive to a friend who lived only a few houses away. The witness told his friend what he had seen, and they went back to the field to see if it was still there.

When they arrived at that location, the huge black cat was indeed still there. They stopped the car and they both ran toward the field. His friend got his camera ready to take a picture. The animal was about eighty yards away and it never looked at them. The animal took off to the bush line and walked into the trees just as the man was about to take a picture. They never saw it again. I received a report of the sighting soon after it had taken place. This area is in the vicinity of the Chestnut Ridge.

CREEPY CRYPTIDS

Stan Gordon

Chapter Seven

Even Stranger Cryptid Incidents

I Swear I Saw a Giant Rabbit – Huntingdon County Early 1960s

Photo of the cutout of the giant rabbit used with permission of the witness.

This was an incident that stayed in the memory of a witness throughout his life. He was a youngster when this adventure took place in the early 1960s. He is certain that this took place. He recalled that family weekend trip for an outing near Spruce Creek in Huntingdon County. He was looking forward to that camping adventure and staying in a small house near a flowing stream.

The witness recalled that he was a passenger in a jeep with some others who were driving down a mountain road for a scenic ride.

CREEPY CRYPTIDS

You could see for miles around from that vantage point. That is when he saw it. It was off to the right about seventy-five to one hundred feet away.

Hopping parallel to the road the witness saw a very large, strange creature that looked like "a dirty white rabbit". He could hardly believe his eyes since this creature looked to be about six feet tall.

The fellow only saw it for seconds from a left side view. The creature moved straight ahead and never looked toward the vehicle. The witness told me he saw the man-sized lepus hopping on its two back legs with its two front paws dangling down in a curled position. Then he lost sight of it as it moved off. He doesn't recall if any of the others saw it that day. He did remember telling a few acquaintances about his experience, but they all laughed at him.

Over the years, some other similar reported sightings of giant rabbits have originated from around the country and elsewhere. I have met this witness in person and we have talked about this several times over the years. He is very credible, and he has no doubt that he saw something very strange many years ago. The witness made a cutout of the huge rabbit and has it in his home to remind him of what he observed as a young boy.

Was There an Even Stranger Mothman Encounter Near Pittsburgh in 1966?

It was in November of 1966 when reports began near Point Pleasant, West Virginia, concerning sightings of a tall, winged humanoid creature with glowing red eyes that was scaring the local residents. It was around that time that I was also hearing rumors that something similar was being seen in Allegheny County around the Pittsburgh area.

Stan Gordon

Sketch of the Pittsburgh area Mothman. Drawing by Rick Rieger

It was years later that I came across a person who had direct knowledge of such events that had taken place in the summer of 1966 in the southern part of Allegheny County.

Those encounters were mentioned in my book, "Astonishing Encounters: Pennsylvania's Unknown Creatures". There had reportedly been a number of encounters with a dark feathery giant creature in a local lovers' lane.

In April of 2010, I met C. William Davis III, a great Pittsburgh mystery book author at the BORU Paranormal Conference in Butler. Bill brought with him a replica of a three toed footprint that he had found near Pittsburgh in the 1950s. I had a display of UFO and Bigfoot material at the conference, and I had a cast of the 3 toed footprint that I found while investigating a Bigfoot case near Greensburg in 1973.

Author C. William Davis III, displays his creation of a three toed footprint he saw in the 1950s in the Pittsburgh area. Stan Gordon (right) shows a picture of a cast of a three toed footprint found near Greensburg, PA in 1973.

Bill later shared with me a personal encounter that had occurred to a close friend of his in 1966, with a creature similar to the Mothman. This incident, however, had taken place in the Pittsburgh area. Bill has written up the following summary of what he recalled about that strange experience from many years ago:

> My name is C. William Davis III. I am a mystery writer, but it is not my books that I would like to talk about. It is an incident that happened early in my life that concerned one of my best friends. It was late fall 1966. It was a weekend evening in a small, southwestern Pennsylvania town along the Allegheny River outside of Pittsburgh. I was attending college in Pittsburgh and was home for the weekend.
>
> My girlfriend Linda who in 1967 was to become my wife and I were sitting in her living room listening to records and talking. As I remember, there was a chill in the air that fall evening.
>
> It was around 10 pm when we heard a knock at the front door. I answered the door and was surprised to see a friend of mine who had told me he would be out on a date. I held the door open and invited him in, but he just stood there with a dazed look on his face. I told him again to come in, but he just continued to stand there staring at me. I quickly realized that something was wrong. I took hold of his arm to help him inside. It was then that I realized his shirt was soaking wet.
>
> Linda and I got him inside and set him down on the couch. He just stared straight ahead and said nothing. He was soaked with sweat, but he felt cold and clammy. As I tried to get some kind of response from him, I also noticed that the left side of his face was red similar to a severe sunburn. Finally, after several minutes we got him to talk but nothing he said made any sense. Linda got up and said, "I'm going to get my mother" and left the room. My friend slowly turned and looked at me and started to cry. He just kept repeating, "I was so scared, I was so scared." I asked,

"Scared of what? Were you in an accident?" I asked again, "Were you in an accident?"

He just looked at me with a stare that showed sheer terror. A look like I had never seen on his face before. When Linda and her mother came into the room, she took one look at him and said, "We need to get him to the dining room and get him warm with a blanket and a hot tea." We tried calling his parents, but we got no answer. We were going to call for an ambulance, but he said "No." He said he was feeling better and just needed to calm down. It was the best part of an hour from the time he came in till he finally began to make sense.

We finally got in touch with his parents who were out, but he had the time to relate what had happened to him before they arrived. He had been dating a local girl for several weeks. On that particular evening they decided to drive to a local dead-end road and go parking. At that time there were no homes in that area. It was in a dark, wooded area on top of a hill that overlooked the area.

He said they had only been there for maybe ten minutes when the car seemed to be bathed in a red glow. At first my friend thought it was the lights from a police car but there was no car in sight. The red glow moved to the driver's side of the car and he said that's when he saw it. He began to tremble again and act as if he was reliving it. It took several minutes to calm him before he continued. What he told us next left us shocked.

He said standing just outside the door was the figure of someone that appeared to be at least eight feet tall. He said it was huge and had red glowing eyes. He said he could feel the heat on his face as it stared at them. He was so scared he could barely hear his girlfriend screaming. He said he wanted to reach for the keys and start the car, but he felt like he couldn't move.

He said the thing just stood there for several minutes and the heat seemed to increase. He said it finally seemed to open its arms as if it had wings and lifted off the ground and over the trees in front of him. He said suddenly the light was gone and his girlfriend stopped screaming. He told us he didn't remember driving her home until he got to her house. He said she screamed at him, "I will never go out with you again."

The next thing he remembered was being on Linda's front porch. His parents finally came and after we talked for several minutes his parents drove him home leaving his car there for the night. His parents took him to the hospital the next day.

He told us they couldn't find anything wrong with him other than the sunburn type redness on the left side of his face. They had no explanation for that other than it appeared to be a radiation burn like sunburn. He talked to me about it again that next day at my parent's house. By then he seemed to be back to normal except for the facial redness which eventually disappeared days later. He seemed to be more concerned about what people thought. Would they think he was crazy? He never spoke much about it after that but when it was brought up, he never denied it and the story never changed.

One year later, December 1967, the same kind of sightings took place not too far away in Point Pleasant, West Virginia. They continued for a period of time with many witnesses coming forth. The sightings seemed to come to a close when the Silver Bridge spanning the Ohio River at Point Pleasant collapsed killing many people. The only comment my friend made was, "I told you what I saw." Linda and I never thought much about it again until a movie came out about the Point Pleasant incident years later.

It was then that we actually believed the connection to that night in the fall of 1966. Over those years Linda and I didn't talk about it much. The times it was brought up my friend would say he remembered but would avoid any lengthy discussion. Unfortunately, my friend, passed away several years ago. When I think back about it now, I know there is no doubt that what he said happened, happened. He was my closest friend and I believe that what he experienced changed a part of his life. Linda and I have mentioned it from time to time but not at great length. We believed him.

Skinny Floating Entity Reported in Butler County August 2015

The following incident took place in late August or the first week of September of 2015. The witness was reluctant to report the encounter when it occurred. I conducted an extensive interview with the observer on September 30, 2015.

The encounter took place on a rural road in eastern Butler County, Pennsylvania, at about 5 PM. It was a sunny day, and the witness was taking a leisurely drive through the scenic area. The driver kept focusing on the road ahead but glanced at a stream to the right of the vehicle and to the woods on the left. Suddenly, about fifteen to twenty feet away and about three quarters of the way across the road, the witness saw something that was hard to describe moving from right to left ahead of the car.

The driver at first thought it was a deer, then quickly realized it was unlike anything that should exist. That was because the first feature that caught the attention of the witness looked similar to the head of a deer. However, the head was angled straight up.

The head was not real pointy. It narrowed at the top then rounded off. The body was similar in color to a deer and appeared very thin and stood between four and four and one half feet tall. The body appeared smooth, and it did not have any apparent hair.

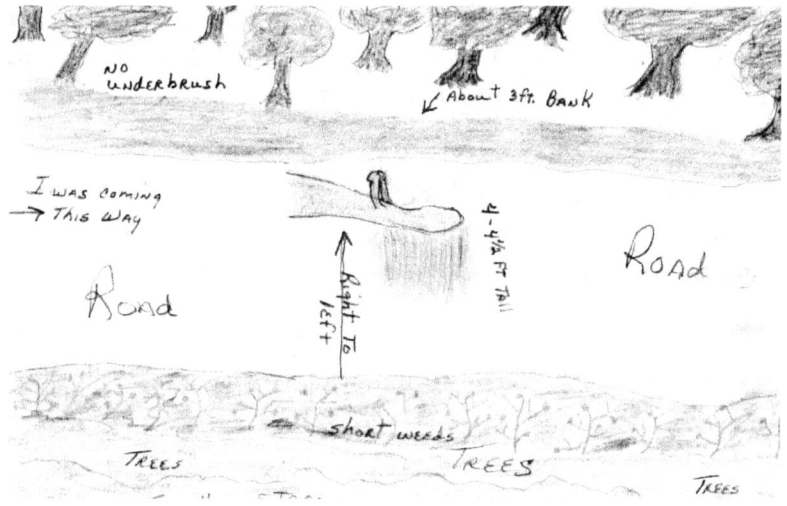

Sketch of skinny floating entity used with permission of the witness.

The being was only observed from the side. It never looked towards the car. No details could be seen on the face. The arms looked to be very short and out of proportion to the rest of the body. The arms were held in very close to the chest area. The hands were very small and gave the impression that they were either being held together or possibly holding something. The witness found it hard to describe, but there appeared to be something hanging down, possibly some type of fabric that was covering around the leg area. No legs or feet were observed.

The driver stated that this being just glided above the roadway. Even stranger was that behind the head an odd effect was noticed. According to the witness, "it looked sort of like a time-lapse picture. Like in a cartoon when the character is moving so fast, the body can't keep up with it." The witness commented, "it looked like the head portion was losing streaks of body matter as it glided across the road."

Within a couple of seconds, the car reached the location on the road where the creature was gliding. The driver looked all around, but the being was nowhere in sight and was not seen again. The witness was stunned and could not understand how this creature could be gone in seconds. The entire observation lasted about seven to eight seconds.

The witness also mentioned that it was unusual that the creature wasn't seen as it came from the right side of the road and was only first seen when it was already gliding ¾ of the way across the road ahead.

Mysterious Over-sized Moth-like Creature Reported in Pennsylvania
July 8, 2017

During 2017, there had been a variety of cryptid reports from across Pennsylvania. Among those incidents that had reportedly occurred were encounters with Bigfoot, black panthers, thunderbirds, and other odd creatures.

The areas around the Allegheny National Forest located in the Northwestern part of Pennsylvania have had a long history of reports of UFOs, Bigfoot, and other mysterious events. On July 8, 2017, a couple who lives near the forest area encountered something that has them baffled. It was about 9 AM that day when the wife went outside to the deck located on the back of their country home. On a post, the woman noticed what looked to be an oversized moth that was resting on a six by six vertical post.

The moth looked to be about eleven inches long and about five and one half inches wide in the area that was described as the shoulders. The overall shape gave the impression of looking like an hourglass figure. They also noticed that there were either two antennas or pointed ears located around the top of the head area that appeared to be about one inch in length. The head appeared to be tucked inside the body while it was resting. The observers estimated that the wingspan would have been around fifteen inches when open.

Drawing used with permission of the witnesses.

The wife called her husband out to also observer the creature. The wife thought that the creature was beautiful, and that the color was a pale green iridescent on the outer part of the wings and a cream color skin texture in the middle. The man said he was amazed at what he saw and had never seen anything like it before.

CREEPY CRYPTIDS

They said the best way to described it was "like an overgrown moth."

They continued to watch the winged creature that appeared to be sleeping. His wife then touched the creature which she said felt smooth. The wings actually felt skin-like, not like feathers or fuzz. The witnesses could not see through the wings. The creature did not move when touched. The woman also noticed that there was no powdery material on her hands that you generally get from coming in contact with the wings of a moth.

The couple had to leave the house for a while. Before they left, his wife went into the house to get a camera to take a picture of the strange, winged visitor. The woman stood about a foot away from the creature and turned on the power switch, but the camera would not turn on. The camera had always worked well so they replaced the batteries. The camera still it would not turn on. The next day they tried the camera again and it powered up as normal and worked fine.

When the couple was walking to their car, they noticed a second similar winged creature resting on the outside wall of their home about ten feet off the ground. When they returned home a while later, both of the creatures had gone.

The couple has provided a sketch of what they saw. The sketch shows the back of the wings and the red area behind it is the six by six vertical post that the creature was resting on vertically.

Addendum: It may just be a coincidence that the camera malfunctioned when the woman attempted to photograph the odd-looking winged creature. However, many years ago, I began to notice some cases where photographic equipment malfunctioned when a person attempted to take a picture of a UFO or other phenomena.

In more recent years, this has been reported in some significant UFO encounters in the state. This phenomenon has also been reported by others involved in paranormal research as well.

Police Officer Encounters Strange Hairless Skinny Creature with Glowing Head
Late August 2017

Sketch used with permission of the witness

On an evening in late August of 2017, a police officer riding down a rural road in a wooded location in southwestern Pennsylvania, saw something that startled him. Ahead of him on the side of the road, the officer observed what appeared to be a ball of very dull white light low to the ground. He was familiar with the area and had never noticed any type of lighting in that location. As he moved closer and was about fifty yards from the round light, it suddenly rose up or stood up from the ground.

It was then that the witness observed something that he couldn't process. The officer told me, "It was the weirdest thing I have ever seen." The ball of light was actually the head of a very strange being that looked to be about six feet tall or larger.

It was tall and almost skeleton thin. The officer was of the opinion that the creature, when he first observed it, had been lying on its belly on the ground, with its head facing toward the road. It then stood up facing the road. In that dark location, he saw the dull light from the glowing head illuminating the upper section of the body of the creature.

While the officer watched, the creature turned toward the right. The dull illumination from the head lit up the shoulder area. The creature then turned and faced him, then turned to the left and took off at an incredible speed away towards a location away from the road. As it moved off, the witness could see its arms swinging.

The officer indicated that it took off at a speed that you could only call abnormal. "It was faster than anything I have ever seen. It was there, then it was gone." The witness assumed that the creature moved on two legs, however, he could not see the lower sections of the body in the dark.

The witness described what he saw as standing six feet or taller. The head was about eight to ten inches in diameter and shaped like a ball. He said the head was just a ball of light, possibly egg shaped but pretty round. The light emitted seemed to be just a dull white. The light illuminated the shoulders, the top of the chest, and a section of the arms.

The officer could not see the hands. The chest looked to be about eighteen inches across. The waist appeared to be small, but the arms were abnormally long. The long limbs also looked skeletal with no muscle mass. The skin tone of the body appeared to be dull grayish blue. The witness could not see any facial features.

The entire experience only lasted about ten seconds. The officer was baffled as to what he saw and about what could move so fast.

He pulled up his vehicle to the location where the creature and been standing and turned on his vehicle spotlight. He looked around the area but saw no evidence on the ground. The officer, after the experience, continued to try to make sense out of what he had encountered but he could not figure it out. I was contacted soon after the incident and we later discussed the incident in detail.

Addendum: While this is a very strange report, many very odd creature encounters have been reported for years from Pennsylvania and all across the country. There have been other reports somewhat similar, and there have been other cases reported where the creature involved had a glowing effect in the dark.

During the many years that I have been investigating such cases in Pennsylvania, I had the opportunity to interview state troopers and municipal police officers who also reported some very strange encounters. In most cases, they spoke with me confidentially about what had taken place.

First a UFO, Then a Close Encounter With a Sickly-Looking Humanoid
September 2017

This very strange incident took place around the middle of September of 2017, in a rural location in northern Westmoreland County. It was around 7:30-8 PM and it was nearing dusk, beginning to darken in the area.

The witness observed an object in the sky that looked like a disc that was rotating with various colored lights that were red, green, blue, and white. The object was bobbing around and there appeared to be an appendage similar to a dangling electrified rope made up of neon lights that was hanging from it.

Soon after seeing the object, a very strange sound emitted from the surrounding woods. The witness was quite familiar with owl sounds and said this was different that it was not an owl. The sound was very loud and steady and more like an "angry noise."

The UFO was still in the sky when several minutes later the witness noticed a figure in the distance approaching from about forty feet away. It was assumed that it was a neighbor, but the witness soon realized that was not the case.

Sketch of the creature used with permission of the witness.

What was seen was a strange being that had a basic human form and stood around five feet eight inches tall. The head of the creature was egg shaped, wider at the top and narrower at the bottom. The color of the creature was odd and gave the impression that it was sickly and in poor health. "It looked to be a very light crème to ivory color."

What frightened the witness even more was that there were no facial features except around what would be the mouth area there seemed to be a wrinkle down one side. The observer saw no eyes, nose, or ears.

The body appeared to be thin and hairless, and wider around the shoulders area, about twenty inches across. The witness could not see any arms or hands. The legs were straight and thin, but they seemed to be bent outward from the knees. It was hard to explain but there appeared to be something odd about the legs. They were separated and one leg seemed to be different than the other one as though it was being dragged.

Even stranger is that from the chest area down to the feet that area of the body seemed to be covered in what was described as "bib overalls" that appeared to be a dark blue or charcoal color. There was little or no neck, and around the chest area, that section of the bib covering seemed to be the same color as the face. The creature made no sound, and no smell was noticed.

The creature seemed to be watching her and a short time after it was seen, some neighbors began to move toward the area. As they got closer, the creature went into the tree line and seemed to suddenly just vanish from sight.

After the people left the area, the creature reappeared about thirty five feet away near the woods. It appeared to be looking toward the observer and it approached the witness steadily and slowly and came to within twenty feet of her. The creature seemed to walk with a slight limp and seemed to be somewhat off balance.

The witness became very frightened, and for a moment was not able to move as a feeling of dread took over. The being seemed to suddenly fade away and disappear and then the witness was able to run to the house and didn't see the creature after that. When last observed, the UFO had dropped down to about one hundred feet where it hovered over the trees. A couple hours later the witness glanced outside but the UFO and creature were not seen again.

Weird Tall Scraggy Hairless Creature Follows Man to His Home
Fall 2018

This very strange encounter occurred during the Fall of 2018 in a very rural location of Armstrong County. The witness, an experienced outdoorsman was in the woods behind his home that evening finishing up some work. He began to hear some sounds in the woods about thirty feet away from him. The steps among the leaves sounded different than the deer he was familiar with that frequented the area. The movement suddenly stopped, then began to become louder.

The witness was familiar with the wildlife in the area, but this seemed different, and he ran back to his house and entered through the back door. He sat down at the dining table in the kitchen that was about five feet from the back door. He was sitting there thinking about what had just occurred up in the woods. He looked toward the glass in the back door and was startled by what he saw.

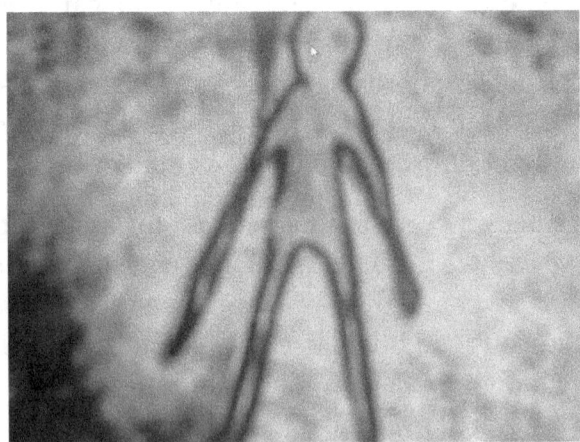

Crouched down at the door was a creature unlike anything he had ever seen before. The humanoid shaped being was on its hands and knees staring directly at the witness. The creature looked like a skeleton covered with all gray skin. The creature was down on its gray bony legs. The legs looked similar to the back legs of a Greyhound dog. The arms were longer than normal, bony, and hairless.

The head was round, and the neck was small. The head appeared to be on its shoulders. The mouth was closed. The eyes of the creature were glowing, a dull yellow color. The man estimated that the creature when standing would be about six to seven feet tall. He could see its spine protruding as it moved.

The witness was stunned by what he was seeing. He immediately spun around to grab for a weapon. When he looked back the creature was down on all fours like a dog and ran along the outside wall of the house. He ran to another window, but he could no longer see it.

It took a long time for this fellow who loved the woods to return back to them. I interviewed the witness in person and found the report very similar to other encounters that were being reported since the Fall of 2017.

Strange Animal Reported Near Latrobe February 2017

In February of 2017, two people were driving down a rural road near Latrobe, PA, when an unusual animal was noticed ahead of them. The incident occurred around 2 AM and the observers had a good look at the mystery animal as it moved through a field.

Whatever it was, it looked to be about the size of a deer and had the build of a greyhound dog. The animal stood about four feet tall, was dark brown in color and was thin and graceful in its movement. The creature had no tail but had a long pointy snout. Note: In the last couple of years, I have been receiving other reports of strange dog-like creatures as well.

Strange, Clawed Footprints Observed in the Snow February 2018

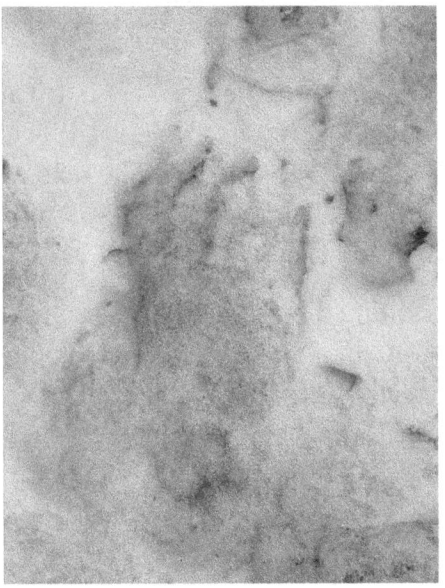

Photo used with permission of the witness.

A series of odd looking clawed footprints were seen in the snow in February of 2018 near Worthington in Armstrong County.

There has been an increase of what appear to be unusual, clawed tracks reported in Pennsylvania and across the country in recent years. These tracks do not appear to be related to dog or cat tracks. There is no doubt, however, that in some cases weather and ground conditions can make normal tracks appear to be unusual.

Misty Humanoid Creature Seen Near Derry September 10, 2018

On the evening of September 10, 2018, a man was riding down a rural road in Derry Township in Westmoreland County. It was a rainy night when his headlights caught something about seventy five feet ahead of him that seemed to "appear out of nowhere". Whatever it was, it was in the middle of the road and was moving from left to right.

The witness said when he first saw this being, he first thought it was fog. He soon realized there was no fog in the surrounding area. The witness said it was hard to describe what he saw, and that it was a humanoid form that was foggy or misty in appearance.

The man stated that it was a "foggy white form" that was about six and one half to seven feet tall. The creature seemed to be somewhat stooped as it moved. The physical traits that stood out to the witness were the huge muscular shoulders and a small waist. There was a head, but he couldn't see it clearly.

The arms and legs were also not clearly discernible. The witness observed the creature from its left side for several seconds. The creature crossed the road and entered into a field where it seemed to just vanish. The man could not see its feet and stated that it moved "almost like it floated". The witness didn't notice any smell or sounds during the observation.

The incident took place only a short distance from the Chestnut Ridge where there has been a long history of UFOs, Bigfoot, and other cryptid encounters.

CREEPY CRYPTIDS

One of the Creepiest Cryptids of All Time: Encounter With a Gigantic Spider in Indiana County 2014

I was contacted by a witness who had an amazing encounter to share. It is one of the weirdest cryptid encounters that I have ever come across.

This person happened to hear me discussing Bigfoot on a radio show in the Pittsburgh area. The witness told me that while I hadn't mentioned the creature that she wanted to tell me about, she thought that I might be able to give her some answers as to what she had encountered.

She said to the best of her memory the incident had taken place during the Spring or Summer of 2014. She lived in a rural section of Indiana County, PA. The woman recalled that she and a friend went outside to do some yard work around her property.

The witness happened to turn around and looked at her home that was about six feet away and was shocked by what she saw. On the side of her house was a door entrance. Crawling up over the door and part of a window near the door was what she could only describe as a "gigantic spider" that was grayish in color.

The door was about six feet tall. The spider was longer than the door. She estimated that the giant arachnid was nearly seven feet in length. What the witness described as the body was about four inches wide. The legs were shiny. The back legs were almost twice the length as the side legs.

She yelled to her friend and questioned what the frightening creature was. They didn't have a working camera at the time to take a picture. They didn't know who to call or what to do.

Stan Gordon

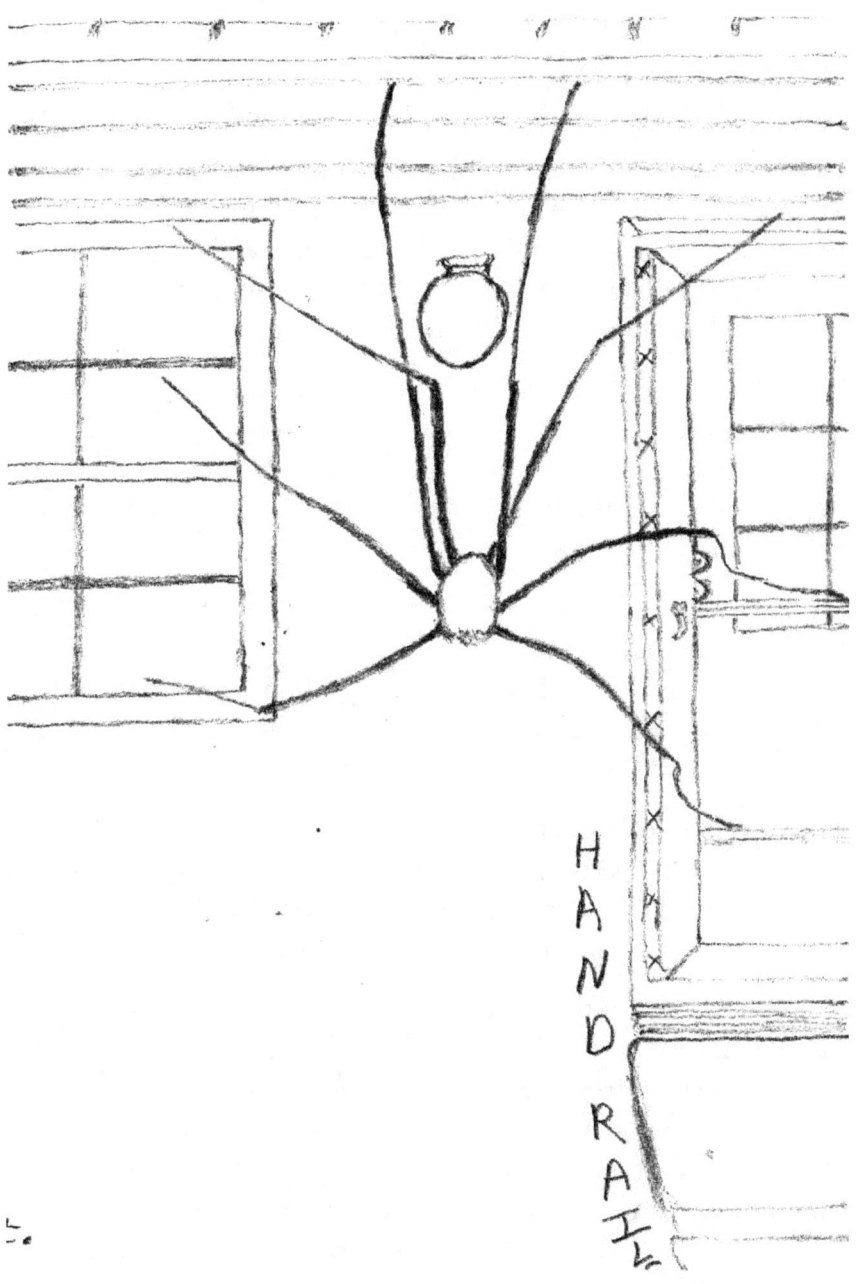

Drawing used with permission of the witness.

CREEPY CRYPTIDS

They both thought that it could be dangerous and that it could harm someone. They decided to kill it and gather up its remains to show other people and to figure out just what this thing was.

Her friend grabbed a sturdy piece of wood to smash the creature. The woman told the man to be sure not to miss hitting it since they didn't know what it would do. He smacked it very hard once or twice in the center of the body. There were marks left on the siding of the trailer where the wood had made contact.

What happened next was even stranger. As soon as the huge spider was struck, the body began to shrivel up. The woman said it looked like an overgrown Daddy Long legs, but then it seemed to suddenly just disappear in front of their eyes as it fell to about a foot from the ground.

The two observers couldn't understand what had happened. They looked all over the ground and around the area, but there was no sign of any fluids, blood, or residue of that huge spider. They kept talking out loud, "it's like it vanished, where did it go?" The woman stated to me "I swear it vanished".

Another odd detail that was also mentioned occurred just as the two people walked outside prior to seeing the huge spider. The environment felt unusual. The woman who lived there recalled that it was a chilly morning with a light fog in the area.

She told me that during the time of the occurrence, the sun was just coming out, but there was also a bright yellow glow that seemed to come from behind the two witnesses and was illuminating the immediate area. The witnesses seemed confused as from where that glow was originating from. The woman told me that the surroundings looked and felt different during the spider encounter. That everything looked beautiful around them, and that it was like being in paradise for a short time.

After the occurrence, the property owner looked up information in a book about spiders in the Pennsylvania and around the country but found out that there were no spiders even close to the size of what they had observed.

The witness also told me that the sketch of the creature on the side of her home was based on where the ends of the legs were located and using the marks on the side of the house where the spider was hit. The legs were drawn into the center. The top of the door to the roof was fifteen inches. It was five feet from the top of the doors to the bottom of the window. The door measured seventy eight inches in length and forty inches wide.

There was about two feet between the door and the window. The light was six inches from the top of the door. The spider itself was estimated to be seventy to eighty inches by fifty inches. The body of the creature seemed smaller than the light. (See drawing above for comparison.)

Addendum: At a later date, I was able to talk with the second witness who saw the gigantic spider. The man confirmed the story and told me that what he saw "was not normal and something very unusual". He said that when they saw the creature and then didn't find any blood or remains after he struck it, they decided to just keep it to themselves since people wouldn't believe them.

The property owner mentioned to me in the years since that strange creepy encounter that a few other mysterious happenings have taken place around that area. Indiana County has a long history of Bigfoot and cryptid encounters.

There are few cases in cryptozoology lore that even mention giant over-sized spiders. The last time I heard of something similar here in Pennsylvania was many years ago in about 1975. I don't recall a lot of detail, but I am sure the reports originated from

Butler County. I remember receiving two separate reports a few days apart.

I still recall those reports because what was supposedly seen was extremely unusual. They were observations of what were described as huge "metallic" spiders crossing a road.

I also have a notation from February of 1975 from Ohio. The report was forwarded to me from a respected researcher from that area. He had received a report of a giant spider that the witness called "Daddy Long-legs" crawling across the road in front of a car. The witness said that it looked like an actual living creature.

Make sure you keep those extra-large cans of insect repellent close by!

Pennsylvania Couple Observe Transparent Creature, Ligonier, PA
November 23, 2015

A husband and wife taking a scenic drive through the Ligonier valley saw something very strange and unexpected on the afternoon of November 23, 2015. At about 2 PM, they were traveling on a rural road about two miles from Ligonier.

The driver of the car noticed some movement in some bushes on the right side of the road. Suddenly, an animal exited the bushes and began to trot from right to left in front of the vehicle. The driver stopped about ten to twenty feet from the animal to obtain a better look. The couple was startled by what they were seeing.

This was no ordinary animal, as they could see the outline of the shape of the animal, but it was not solid and there was no color or fur observed. The husband, as soon as he saw the creature, thought that it was somewhat like a fox but could not be sure since no physical features could be seen. His wife also agreed that it was a four-legged creature similar to a fox.

The body of the animal was estimated to be about eighteen inches to twenty-four inches long and had a tail that was about one fourth to one half the length of the body. The animal was a lot smaller than a deer.

The husband told me that the creature had a "smoky veil shape". His wife, however, got a better and longer look at the animal as it entered the road and trotted in front of the car. She told me that she could "see through it," and that there was a specific area within the body shape that was like an energy pattern. "It was like a smoky heatwave."

They watched as the animal continued to cross the road and entered some brush on the left side of the road and was not seen again. The couple didn't hear any sound or notice any smell during the four to five second observation.

Small Alien-looking Humanoid Creature Seen In the Headlights of a Passing Car
July 5, 2019

Sketch of the small humanoid used with permission of the witness.

A motorist traveling on a rural road not far from Youngwood noticed something unusual. About fifteen feet away stepping out from a section of bushes along the road was a four to five foot tall hairless humanoid creature.

The being was very thin and had an oval shaped head. It had a long skinny neck, and the eyes were black and appeared to be elliptical like that of a cat.

The witness only saw it for a few seconds and only from the one side. He was not able to see any arms or feet. The legs were very thin. It did have what appeared to be a protruding belly.

As soon as the headlights illuminated the area where the creature was standing, the being quickly moved back into the bushes. The man did not see it again.

Dark Gliding Unknown Being Crosses Field May 2020

During late May of 2020, a witness was getting some fresh air and listening to the car radio. This incident took place at a rustic location a few miles away from the Donegal area. The eyewitness was watching several deer in a field across the road. It was dark outside, but the field had some slight illumination.

Suddenly something frightened the deer and they quickly ran out of the area. Moments later, a tall figure was seen crossing the field. The figure had a humanoid shape and appeared to be very dark. It was difficult to see any physical details, however, the witness noticed that the arms of the entity looked bent and were not swinging as it moved. The observer estimated at that distance that the creature appeared to be over six feet tall.

It was it's movement that was so unusual. The witness explained to me that whatever this creature was, it did not appear to be running like a normal person. It seemed as though it was actually gliding across the field. It moved extremely fast crossing about seventy five yards in ten seconds. The strange being was soon lost from sight.

The witness has no idea as to what this creature was but is certain that it was not human.

Addendum: During my many years of investigations, I have received other reports of strange creatures that have been observed gliding or floating over roadways and fields. While this observation startled the witness, this is not a unique report. Other people have reported something similar.

It Was Very Tall and Ran Faster Than Any Human August 2020

It was on a nice day in August of 2020 that this witness decided to take a hike through a wooded area of Jefferson County a few miles from Cook Forest. The man started his journey that afternoon and was looking forward to a relaxing trek through the woodlands. The weather was clear and the temperature was comfortable when he arrived at the location.

The hiker had made his way deeper into the woods when he entered a small valley. The man was looking ahead when he noticed something that caught his attention about one hundred to two hundred feet in the distance. What he saw was a very tall figure standing between two trees. The area where this took place was quite dense and not close to public access, so he was surprised that anyone else would be in the area.

As the hiker continued to watch, he quickly realized that what he was seeing was not a person, deer, or even a black bear. The creature – whatever it was – stepped to the right of the observer and moved to its left in front of a tree. The witness could now see the landscape between those two trees as that area was no longer hidden by the tall figure.

That figure then took off running extremely fast down the hillside to its left, so it was not moving in the direction of the witness. The man told me that the creature moved faster than any human could possibly run. What was even more unusual, he could not hear any sound as it ran through the foliage and rocks. The entire encounter lasted only about a minute or two. It was enough time for the witness to see some details.

CREEPY CRYPTIDS

The man estimated that the creature stood between eight to ten feet tall, and the general shape of the shadow figure/ person was distinct. The arms and legs were long and narrow; almost boxy looking. The creature was positioned at a forty five degree angle towards him. He could not tell the length of the arms or legs. He did notice that arms appeared to be bent at about a twenty degree angle and held out straight. The arms were not swinging as it moved.

While he did not notice any hair or fur on the body, an interesting detail was that the entire time he saw the creature, it looked as though it was out of focus. It looked, "fuzzy", "blurry", or "smokey". The face was indistinct, but he was able to see a head.

The witness did not notice any odd sounds or smells while the observation took place. The man told me that he is speculating that the creature was surprised to see him and when it did it quickly ran off.

The witness told me that he has the image of that creature taking off and running seared into his mind. He also commented that he has told very few people about what he saw, and he stated, "I know exactly what I saw". The witness has never seen anything strange during his walks through the woods and will always wonder what he saw that August afternoon.

Addendum: There are other witnesses I interviewed that have seen Bigfoot and who have described the appearance of the creature as out of focus, or misty or foggy in appearance. This adds to the mystery as to what Bigfoot might really be. Just what did the witness see? A Bigfoot- or did he see some other type of strange entity?

Stan Gordon

Chapter Eight

The Mysterious Chestnut Ridge and the Laurel Highlands of Pennsylvania

A section of the Chestnut Ridge near Derry, Pennsylvania, where over the years, many Bigfoot sightings and other phenomena have been reported.

It was during an investigation of a daylight UFO sighting in 1969, when I first began to hear about the strange occurrences that were taking place in locations along the Westmoreland County section of the Chestnut Ridge.

I immediately made contact with the people involved after receiving the report and went to the location of the sighting. I would also later meet with other observers as well.

CREEPY CRYPTIDS

At the time of the incident, it was a beautiful afternoon, and the sky was clear and absent of any clouds. The UFO sighting had taken place near the intersection of Route 119 and Route 22 not far from Blairsville. The family in the car had slowed down as they approached a construction crew working along the highway.

One of the passengers called out to look up in the sky. That is when they all noticed an object hovering over the top of some trees. They sat there in their car for about five minutes trying to figure out what the object was. At first, they thought it was a blimp, but soon realized it was much stranger. The large solid object was very bright white in color and shaped like a long wide oval. The object did not appear to have a shiny surface. The observers did not notice any sound while the object was being observed.

The object appeared at first to be hovering over a short distance over the trees. Then the object began to drop lower and moved a short distance toward the right and hovered again. The object moved slow and steady as though it was moving down steps. The object then continued to move even lower and toward the right again. Then the object dropped lower and appeared to go down below the trees and was lost from sight. It gave the impression that it might be going to land.

The witnesses couldn't believe what they had seen. They had heard the stories from people who claimed to have seen strange objects in the sky, but they had always dismissed those accounts. They drove to the area where the object appeared to have lowered toward the ground but saw nothing. They then returned to the location where they had originally observed it from. Once again, the object was no longer in sight. They were so intrigued by what had taken place that they called the state police.

When I went to the scene, I searched the wooded area where the object reportedly went down but I found no evidence of anything unusual. During the next couple of days after the incident, I talked with some other local residents, but none were aware of the sighting.

There was one witness in the area, however, who stated that about that time and on the same day he heard an unusual sound. He described it as a loud buzzing that was followed by two explosive sounds that seemed to originate from above his house. He went outside but saw nothing and had no idea what the sounds had originated from.

As I talked with more local residents, some of them began sharing stories with me of tales of mysterious lights, large hair covered upright creatures, underground sounds and even an entrance that supposedly opened in the side of the Chestnut Ridge somewhere around Derry Township.

In the years since then I have interviewed scores of witnesses who have had strange experiences around the Chestnut Ridge. The ridge area extends through sections of Westmoreland, Fayette, and Indiana counties in southwestern Pennsylvania and continues to near Morgantown, West Virginia into Preston County. Reports such as that of UFOs, Bigfoot, various other strange creatures, and other anomalies continue to be reported yearly from nearby localities.

While incidents have been reported from throughout the region, some of the locations where incidents have commonly been reported from include, Derry Township, Latrobe, Youngstown, and the Ligonier Valley area in Westmoreland County. There have been frequent reports from near Ohiopyle, Dunbar, Fairchance and the Uniontown area in Fayette County. Other incidents have taken place near Homer City and Blairsville and other sections of Indiana County as well.

CREEPY CRYPTIDS

Many encounters have been reported from the forests, and woodlands of Pennsylvania as well as state parks. For example, many very strange incidents have reportedly taken place in the vicinity of Forbes Forest, Linn Run, and Keystone state parks.

While I have focused on the many anomalies that have taken place historically along the Chestnut Ridge located on the western side of the Allegheny Mountain range, numerous other unusual occurrences have been reported throughout the nearby Laurel Ridge area as well.

In this book and in my three previous books, you will learn about peculiar cases that are said to have taken place throughout the Chestnut Ridge and also the Laurel Highlands region. The Laurel Highlands spreads through sections of Westmoreland, Fayette, and Somerset counties.

The phenomena reported in these locations are not new to those who have lived there over many years. I interviewed a witness that lived near Indianhead in Fayette County who reported that a large hair covered Bigfoot type creature would on occasion visit their farm in 1931.

In the summer of 1954, a seven-foot-tall hair covered creature was seen near Latrobe strolling near a wooded area. On a nearby farm, tall rows of corn were broken, and strange footprints were seen.

Some of the puzzling accounts reported from this region have been close range sightings of large mysterious objects in the sky and encounters with small solid or luminous mini-UFOs that came close to the witnesses.

There have been encounters with Bigfoot, Thunderbirds, black panthers, and other strange creatures. Locals have reported mystery booms, underground sounds, tree anomalies, ghosts and apparitions, odd electromagnetic effects, strange sounds and smells, various types of unusual footprints and other tracks. Portals, odd weather phenomena, peculiar animal reactions, and the feeling of overpowering fear in some locations. There are even accounts of mysterious men who seemed to have an interest in some very high strangeness cases that occurred in these areas.

In this chapter and throughout this book, you will be reading about some of the very strange incidents reported around the Chestnut Ridge and the Laurel Highlands.

A Tree Inside Another Old Tree on the Ridge Fall 2011

In the Fall of 2011, I was contacted by a resident who lived on the Chestnut Ridge in Westmoreland County. The family often took walks on their property and they were very familiar with the trees and other landmarks throughout the area. On one of their recent outings, they noticed something that looked quite odd, and they couldn't find a good explanation for what they had discovered.

They soon contacted me, and I arrived in the area along with a small group of other investigators. There was a tall maple tree that had been on the property for many years. The landowners had commonly walked near it many times, but on this occasion, they noticed something unusual. What they saw was not apparent in more recent excursions.

About twenty feet up in the tree there was a hollowed-out section that had been noticeable for a long time. It was what was seen in the hollowed-out area inside the tree that was so unusual.

There was another tree that looked to be still alive and positioned upside down inside of the older larger tree. The roots of that smaller tree were extending up toward the top. There was no indication of the smaller tree having originated from the immediate area. We also checked for any type of weather damage in the area such as a microburst, but there was no indication of anything like that having taken place in that location. It was an interesting mystery.

Stan near the hollowed out tree on the ridge.

Bright Glow Observed Over the Chestnut Ridge August 26, 2012

Just before 9 PM on the evening of August 26, 2012, a witness from the Latrobe area was looking toward the Chestnut Ridge. In the direction of Indiana County, he observed a very bright glow in the sky that lasted about three seconds. The flash was yellow green in color and took up a large section of the sky.

The Boulder in a Tree On Top of the Chestnut Ridge

Picture used with permission of Dwayne Pintoff.

Dwayne Pintoff and Tom Ference have had an interest in Bigfoot sightings in Pennsylvania for many years. They have traveled to various locations in Westmoreland and Fayette Counties to look for evidence of these elusive unknown creatures. It was in October of 2013, when these two local researchers were exploring the Chestnut Ridge in the Derry area when they came across another anomaly that baffled them.

They were quite surprised to see a boulder lying in a tree at the top of the ridge. The boulder was resting in the branch of a tree that was about fifty to sixty feet tall and was located between two protruding rock ledges. The tree was located at the top of a forty to fifty foot high hillside. The researchers used a tape measure and determined that the tree was about eight feet from the ledge.

A rough measurement of the boulder indicated that it was about 30"x 18" X 2" in size. The two men weren't certain if the boulder was made of granite or sandstone, but they estimated that it weighed between sixty five to ninety pounds. At a later date, it was determined that the boulder was actually made of sandstone, so that weight would likely have been around sixty pounds.

In the report of the incident that Dwayne submitted to me, he commented that both he and Tom still didn't know who could have placed or thrown a boulder of that size into a tree at that height and distance from where someone would have been standing to put it there. It remains another Chestnut Ridge mystery.

Unusual Object Photographed During Storm Near the Laurel Ridge in Pennsylvania
April 2020

On the evening of April 7, 2020, Ronald Shawley had setup his tripod and camera to take photos of an intense lightning storm that was moving through Cambria and Indiana counties in Pennsylvania. Ron is an experienced photographer and a certified storm chaser. Ron was using a Canon EOS Rebel T5i camera and taking some pictures as the storm was passing nearby.

It was when Ron was reviewing the pictures that he had taken that evening when he noticed something unusual. What Ron saw he could not easily explain. He is familiar with many of the strange cloud formations that are described in meteorological records. He has seen many pictures that looked unusual but had technical explanations.

Ron is baffled by what appears to be one or more objects followed by a long misty trail located along the bottom center in the picture. The visual phenomena he recorded looks to be at low altitude in the vicinity of the Laurel Ridge.

Stan Gordon

Picture used with permission of Ronald J. Shawley.

Ron Shawley suggested a theory that the strange object he photographed could have been phasing in and out and might have been from an inter-dimensional source. The appearance of the object was enhanced by the energy from the very heavy lightning storm that was close by.

Addendum: The reports I have received indicate that strange activity is also quite active in areas beyond the Chestnut Ridge at locations near and along the Laurel Ridge as well. I have had multitudes of unusual incidents reported from throughout the Laurel Highlands.

Creepy Cryptids

Stan Gordon

Chapter Nine
Other Unusual Occurrences

Mystery Booms Reported in Southwestern PA in 2018

For many years, there have been reports of very loud mystery booms that have shaken homes and rattled the windows of structures. In the 1960's we used to call these events "Sky Quakes". These loud earth shakings have been going on for years around southwestern Pennsylvania and across the state and around the country as well.

In some cases, there have been explanations for these occurrences. Some of these loud sounds were determined to be associated with sonic booms, fireball meteors passing over an area, and local blasting, There have been various other theories proposed concerning these incidents including a meteorological event known as a "frost quake". In some cases, these mystery shakings have not been explained.

I have been receiving reports of some recent loud booms from northern and central locations in Westmoreland County. During the week of January 21, 2018, I became aware of two such incidents.

CREEPY CRYPTIDS

A Very Strange Deer Mutilation in the Laurel Highlands June 18, 2019

I received this report from a very reputable businessman who lives in a wooded location in the Laurel Highlands. On the morning of June 18, 2019, the witness had awakened early and was putting out some trash when he looked ahead in the distance at the driveway. On his driveway was the carcass of a dead deer.

What he saw baffled him. The top section of the animal's body was untouched. The head and front legs of the animal were also intact. It was the bottom section of the deer's body that drew his attention. The entire lower section of the carcass was missing. There were no intestines, bones, or blood, which baffled the man.

The witness returned to that location about an hour later to clean up the mess from his driveway. When he returned, he had another surprise. The rest of the upper section of the deer carcass that had been untouched was now completely gone. There was only a small amount of intestines on the ground. There was also no blood seen around the carcass. The witness was baffled by the condition of the animal's body.

Addendum: There has been a history of mysterious cattle mutilations that have occurred across the country since the 1960s. These types of reports are rarely reported in Pennsylvania or this part of the country. During the many years of my investigations, I have only heard of a small number of unusual animal mutilations in Pennsylvania that mainly involved cattle and dogs. In some instances, there may have been explanations for what reportedly took place.

Stan Gordon

CHAPTER TEN

BIGFOOT AND CRYPTID MYSTERIOUS FINDINGS

During my many years of conducting in the field investigations of UFOs, Bigfoot and cryptid encounters, my view has changed quite a bit concerning the reality of what it is that we might be dealing with concerning these anomalies that continue to be reported.

When I started my research in 1959 as a ten-year-old youngster and later became an active field investigator in 1965, I realized from the reports that came to my attention, that many of these sightings and encounters could indeed by explained. Many UFO sightings and even cryptid encounters were misidentifications of natural or man-made objects.

As more of these strange sighting crossed my desk, it became evident that some detailed accounts from credible observers could not be explained away so easily. It was during the earlier years of UFO research that myself and other researchers were of the opinion that some of these sightings of strange aerial phenomena were likely the spacecraft of extraterrestrial visitors.

Since at least the late 1940s throughout this country, there were numerous incidents where witnesses reported seeing what appeared to be large solid or luminous objects in the sky. In some cases, these objects were low to the ground. There were reports of these objects hovering over roadways, pacing vehicles, and there were even landing cases where witnesses- on occasion- also reported observing humanoid creatures that were generally small in stature.

Bigfoot encounters had been reported throughout the country for many years. I had heard of sightings taking place in Pennsylvania during the 1960s and I spoke with people who told me of their encounters during that period of time. In those days, I was convinced that some of those reports seemed authentic and that Bigfoot was apparently an animal species that was unknown to science.

It was in 1972 when a series of unusual events were reported by local residents outside of Greensburg, Pennsylvania, that I began to notice some odd details that these people were sharing with me. The incidents were taking place around a large, normally quiet wooded area.

The locals began to report loud screams and howls, and heavy bipedal sounds of something large prowling nearby. Some homeowners reported seeing strange footprints, a large husky creature chasing dogs, and strange small lights close to the ground and other UFO sightings around the general area.

It was during the immense wave of UFO and Bigfoot sightings that took place in Pennsylvania in 1973, that many very strange and significant encounters took place. Some of those unusual occurrences continued into 1974 as well. That is when I began to realize that the Bigfoot and UFO phenomena was considerably more unusual than what I was aware of and had considered in my earlier years of research. My thoughts concerning the UFO and Bigfoot phenomena began to change.

These types of extraordinarily strange cases have continued to be reported during the years since that time. I also became aware from my conversations and contacts with other researchers as well as witnesses that similar incidents had been taking place across the United States and other countries as well.

It became apparent to me since the early 1970s, that some Bigfoot researchers were aware of cases that involved both Bigfoot and UFOs but were reluctant to talk about those cases since they were so unusual, and the researchers were fearful that they would be rejected by their associates.

In regard to the cases I have investigated in past years that concerned incidents involving a UFO sighting with a Bigfoot encounter at the same time and place, let me be clear. I am not saying that Bigfoot is a passenger or crew member of a spacecraft from another planet. There may well be more than one origin concerning the unknown category of UFO phenomena. Some of the theories that have been proposed by various researchers over the years include extraterrestrial spacecraft, inter-dimensional visitors, time travelers, unknown atmospheric phenomena, and demons.

In more recent years others involved in Bigfoot research around the country are now talking about similar strange cases that have come to their attention.

I am going to share with you some of the strange details that have come to my attention during my investigations of some Bigfoot and cryptid encounters.

- In most cases Bigfoot has been estimated to range in height from six to nine feet tall, covered in hair, and appears to be a solid physical creature. There are also encounters with small Bigfoot creatures that are estimated to be in the range of four to five feet tall. There have also been some variations in the physical descriptions of some of these creatures. Some, for example, have been taller and thinner. There have been cases reported where a Bigfoot-like creature was estimated to be closer to twelve feet tall.

- In some instances, the body of the creature observed appeared to be out of focus, or misty or foggy yet the shape could be seen. Sometimes only a section of the body looked solid and other parts were not in focus. There were cases where the creature ran off and only certain sections of its body were visible. There are various other cryptid encounters reported where the witness described the creature as having a shimmering appearance to it.

- Many witnesses have described the long stride and extreme pace as a Bigfoot ran away. In contrast, there are cases where the creature appears to glide or float over the terrain rather than running. (Other cryptids are reported to do this as well.)

- There are other reports where a Bigfoot was observed at a location not far from a witness. Suddenly, the creature would physically vanish, and seconds later reappear in another nearby position.

- In some cases, hunters, outdoorsmen and other witnesses have reported an overpowering fear when in the vicinity of a Bigfoot.

- My teams would respond to locations where a Bigfoot had been seen. In some cases, there would be trails of footprints that would suddenly just end abruptly with no explanation. This occurred with various ground conditions including fresh snow. This has continued to be reported even in recent years by other witnesses around the country.

- The typical five toed footprints associated with Bigfoot have been reported for years in Pennsylvania and around the country. There have also been many three toed and four toed tracks reported in Pennsylvania as well as other states. Throughout the country in areas that have a long history of Bigfoot sightings, three toed tracks have also been reported where five toed tracks are also common.

Over the years, there have been some hoaxed Bigfoot tracks in cases I investigated. These tracks were quite often easily discernible. There were other tracks reported over the years that were determined to be bear tracks or tracks of other wild animals that looked unusual due to various weather conditions.

There is, however, a larger mystery concerning the footprints associated with Bigfoot sightings in Pennsylvania. Besides the five and three toed tracks, a number of other very strange footprints have been found over the years in different locations across the state. The cases were investigated and there was no indication of hoaxing taking place. The overall shapes and toe configuration, and sizes of the tracks were unusual. Some of these cases were investigated by other Bigfoot researchers as well.

The existence of these tracks adds even more mystery to the Bigfoot phenomena. It is strange enough that the data suggests that we have been dealing with one unknown hairy bipedal creature, but to think that there could be multiple species of unknown Bigfoot-like creatures strolling across the country is hard to wrap your head around. There are, however, so many credible witnesses that we can't just dismiss these reports.

The same goes for the numerous out of place black panther encounters. Then we have the Thunderbirds of various sizes and descriptions, Dogman, floating entities, winged humanoids, mysterious aquatic creatures, tall skinny hairless humanoids, hooded and small gnome-like beings, and countless other odd entities. Once again, there are so many very credible witnesses who have provided similar detailed reports that you can't just pretend that these cases don't exist.

CREEPY CRYPTIDS

This is a cast of a three toed footprint that was made on August 7, 1973, in a rural area outside of Greensburg, PA. I found the track on a hill up behind a house where a man, who was shaving, saw something with large glowing red eyes staring at him through a bathroom window that was eight feet off the ground.

I have interviewed hundreds of Bigfoot witnesses since the 1960s. They are men, women, and children of various backgrounds and age groups. Most of the witnesses didn't believe the stories they had heard about Bigfoot until they had their own encounter. One thing that many of the witnesses had in common was that they wanted no publicity. This also applies to the many people who have encountered cryptids and other mystery beasts. Outdoorsmen, experienced hunters, teachers, engineers, and police officers are among the eyewitnesses.

- Most Bigfoot sightings commonly take place in or near wooded and forested areas. There are many cases of these creatures walking out in front of vehicles on rural roads that are surrounded by woods. They have also been reported near mobile homes and other dwellings in wooded areas as well.

- There has been an increase in Bigfoot encounters taking place in more populated areas and even near towns and cities where there are little or no woods nearby.
- Many Bigfoot encounters take place in daylight and many cases have occurred at close range.
- Bigfoot appears to have a curiosity about human activities.
- The creatures at times have thrown large rocks and tree branches at witnesses that were nearby. They have at times approached towards people then moved off and left the area. People have commented that if these creatures wanted to hurt them, they could have easily done so.
- UFOs and Bigfoot have made appearances in the same areas within a short time frame.
- There have been documented cases of UFOs and Bigfoot seen together at the same time and place.
- In one case a Bigfoot was carrying a small sphere of light as it ran towards a wooded area.
- Bigfoot and small spheres of light and other odd light phenomena have been reported in the same areas. This has been reported many times throughout the country by Bigfoot investigators in areas that have a history of Bigfoot sightings.
- There are reports of balls of light changing into various cryptids.
- There are people who say they have seen various creatures transform into another physical form.

CREEPY CRYPTIDS

- A Bigfoot suddenly vanished in a flash of light after being fired upon at close range with a shotgun.

- There have been incidents reported where witnesses have seen brilliant flashes of light close to the ground or near locations where cryptid and other unusual activity had taken place. The weather conditions were clear at the time and no sound was heard.

- Bigfoot was shot at with various firearms and the creature reportedly just vanished from sight or the creature appeared unharmed and continued to exit the area.

- Bigfoot suddenly appearing into view then vanishing from sight.

- Witnesses in some locations have described portals or doorway, or as in one case a tube-like device where debris from the ground was swirling and being sucked up into it. There have been some theories that these are some types of gateways where these mysterious flying objects and creatures come and go between other dimensions.

- Witnesses who were able to get a good look at these creatures have reported that in some cases the eyes appeared to be self-luminescent and glowing brightly. In most cases, there was no moon light or artificial lighting in the area to cause such an effect. The eye colors commonly reported were red or orange while some observers described it as a reddish-orange. Glowing yellow and green eyes have also been reported.

- I have had incidents reported when a creature would turn its head and the eye color would change from a luminous red to green color. Witnesses who saw a Bigfoot in daylight have commented how brilliant the eyes were. In other cases, the eyes are not luminous at all, and some witnesses have described them as very dark or black and piercing.

Stan Gordon

- During the 1973-1974 Bigfoot sightings, my teams would examine nearby caves or mines if a Bigfoot encounter had taken place in that vicinity. We saw no evidence that such a creature was sheltering in them.

- Bigfoot is capable of emitting various loud vocalizations. Some witnesses described the intense amplitude of the sounds to be so abnormal that it vibrated through their bodies. Some of the sounds reported have been a baby crying, a woman in pain screaming, a high-pitched whistle, a very heavy breathing sound, various whoops, and screams.

- There have been reports in recent years describing the sound as though it was from a giant owl. There have also been reports of a sound similar to monkey chatter. There have been reports from some people that have heard what appears to be multiple different animal sounds during the same loud continuous vocalization. These creatures appear to have the ability to mimic other animal sounds as well as human sounds.

- This is rarely discussed, but there are cases where a Bigfoot has walked near a car causing the vehicle to lose power. As the creature moved away, the car once again operated normally. Similar Electromagnetic Effect cases have occurred when UFOs have hovered near passenger vehicles and the engine failed or in some cases the headlights dimmed. Radio interference has also been reported.

- Witnesses have attempted to photograph a UFO only to find that their camera device malfunctioned at that time but worked normally after the incident. There have been similar cases related to cryptid encounters as well.

- There are reports of Bigfoot seen together with another type of cryptid at the same time and place.

- There have been many accounts of loud thuds or bangs that appear to hit against the side of houses or mobile homes in areas of Bigfoot activity. There have been cases of Bigfoot moving on the roofs of low structures as well. Some witnesses have reported an odd metallic sound when a Bigfoot was nearby.

- There were incidents where a witness had a very close encounter with a Bigfoot. That person left that location and traveled several miles after being so frightened. Within the hour, the same or a similar Bigfoot showed up at that second location.

- In some instances, Bigfoot witnesses have reported a very strong smell associated with the appearance of the creature. The odor has been commonly described a similar to rotten eggs or sulfur, or an animal that has been dead for quite a while. On the other hand, there are many Bigfoot encounters reported where there is no smell. I am of the opinion that the odor might be related to the process of how these creatures move in and out of our physical reality.

- I would not exclude the possibility that there could be a species of Bigfoot that science still has not been able to confirm. But if this is so, why have sightings of similar creatures been reported for years and years all across the globe and still no body has been found and verified?

- There are some details that have been coming to my attention that suggests that in some cases the local immediate area and possibly the individuals nearby, are temporarily manipulated in various odd ways in locations where a cryptid or other anomalist encounter has taken place. I am calling these incidents, Environmental Physical Anomalies.

- At times, an outbreak of various anomalistic incidents seems to target a specific geographical location. Residents begin to report strange incidents such as UFO sightings, loud howls and whoops from the woods, bright balls of light, mysterious footprints, Bigfoot and other cryptid encounters, apparitions, and other paranormal phenomena.

- In some cases, these incidents can continue on for days, weeks, months, or even years. I first noticed this phenomenon taking place during the early 1970s and I began to write about my findings at that time. Since then, other similar anomalous outbreaks have taken place in Pennsylvania and other locations across the country. I have previously mentioned the localized outbreak of strange occurrences that took place near Greensburg, PA in 1972.

During that massive wave of UFO and Bigfoot activity that took place from 1973 into 1974, many of those cases seemed to focus on certain areas along and near the Chestnut Ridge which is located in Westmoreland, Fayette, and Indiana counties in Pennsylvania. Additionally, there were numerous other strange incidents taking place in other locations across the state. The Chestnut ridge area continues to be active yearly with UFO and cryptid reports.

It was in 1979 near Apollo, Pennsylvania, that a long series of mysterious occurrences began about two weeks after a strange object tumbled from the sky one afternoon. The residents around the area were seeing not only Bigfoot but also black panthers as well. They were hearing various strange sounds and seeing strange small round lights in a field. Witnesses said these small lights were so bright they would illuminate the surrounding trees. Large footprints were seen in the snow that suddenly just ended.

One evening a home was encompassed in a brilliant white light. The dogs and other animals were frightened at times during the ongoing incidents. Another incident occurred where a horse was so frightened it broke through an electric fence. Tree branches were found strangely twisted. People in the area were reporting bright flashes of light near the ground. This series of events went on for several years and was covered on Pittsburgh television and in the local newspaper.

It is rare in Pennsylvania cases, yet a small number of witnesses have reported that Bigfoot seemed to attempt to mentally communicate with them. There was one case that I can confirm since I was on the scene when such an incident took place. A witness stated at that time that the creature had communicated that a UFO incident would take place the next morning about fifteen miles away in another county. A strange incident did indeed occur the next morning over the town that was mentioned. The local fire department actually responded to this occurrence and it made the local news.

CONCLUSION

A Phenomena Beyond Our Present Scientific Understanding

There are some very unusual cases discussed in this book which indicates that some of the strange creatures being reported have characteristics that suggest that they are not just unknown species and may not be of flesh and blood. Based on information that I have accumulated from around Pennsylvania and around the country and elsewhere, it seems that Bigfoot, at times, and certain other cryptids can suddenly appear out of nowhere and then disappear.

There are cases where these creatures have changed their physical form into something else. Balls of light have reportedly changed into other creatures. Footprints being followed have changed into other types of tracks. There seems to be a physical and non-physical component related to some of these incidents. It has become apparent to me from the numerous accounts that I have investigated that there is an energy correlation with these cases as well.

One detail that has commonly turned up for years here in Pennsylvania is that many, low level, close range UFO encounters, and many Bigfoot, Thunderbird, black panther, and other cryptid incidents commonly take place near sources of energy. These mysterious encounters occur near high tension power lines, power plants, radio and cell phone towers, gas lines and gas wells, windmill farms, railroad tracks, bodies of water and reservoirs, fuel storage sites, etc.

I have investigated multitudes of UFO reports in past years. In many cases these were daylight observations that were at close range and at low level. In some cases, these objects would suddenly just appear.

CREEPY CRYPTIDS

There were incidents where these objects appeared to be physically solid and then would suddenly begin to fade away and disappear- just vanishing from sight. There are other reports where these objects physically changed shape in front of the observers. In one case, for example, the shape transformed from a sphere into a large rectangular object. In most cases, there was no sound during these observations. In some cases what appeared to be solid objects entered clouds but never exited from them. There are also reports of people seeing just the solid outline of a large object moving across the sky, but they could see through it.

There are some similarities with what UFO witnesses have reported and with some Bigfoot and other cryptid cases as well. Some Bigfoot witnesses have described the creature just suddenly appearing then disappearing from sight. Witnesses unknown to each other have used similar terms when describing their experiences such as "It was there then it was gone" or "It was like watching a Predator movie".

Some of the strange creatures being reported might indeed be specimens of animals that science has not confirmed. There are other cryptids, however, that have attributes that do not appear to be those of a flesh and blood animal.

I noticed a detail from witnesses of various cryptids in more recent years that I think is fascinating. Some of these people were quite close to these strange beasts and they mentioned that once the creature realized that it was being observed by a human, it either look startled or reacted as though it was frightened and quickly exited the area.

A witness to one very bizarre cryptid encounter in 2012, told me that the creature showed a horrific expression, like it was panicked, and took a deep breath when it realized it was being seen.

These creatures seem to feel safe being in the vicinity of humans as it seems that they feel they are not detected by us, so does something occur at times that interferes with this veil of protection that allows us to see them? This startled reaction is not common with many of the cryptid encounters but has been brought up at times.

Since the 1970s, I have been aware of some incidents that indicated that the government has had a long interest in investigating not only the UFO phenomena, but also the Bigfoot mystery. I have held the opinion for a long time that our government knows a lot more about UFOs than they are revealing to the general public. The government likely knows more about Bigfoot and maybe some other cryptids as well. I think it is quite likely that they are also trying to understand more about these ongoing mysterious incidents and to learn how and why they occur.

In regard to the UFO mystery, I don't think the government has the answers either and they are likely finding that this ongoing phenomenon far exceeds our current technology and that the answers to solving this mystery is beyond our current scientific understanding.

The more I have learned about these various anomalies, the more likely it seems that many of the unknown aerial phenomena and mini-UFOs, mysterious beasts, and other paranormal occurrences appear to be somehow related and are a part of the same originating source, whatever that may be. They could possibly be inter-dimensional. They are both physical and non-physical at times, and they come, and they go. They are here and then they are gone.

We must keep an open mind as these encounters will continue to take place in the months and years ahead. As I stated years ago, "The phenomenon is so strange it protects itself".

Creepy Cryptids

Stan Gordon

About the Author

Stan Gordon began his interest in the UFO subject and other strange occurrences at the age of ten in 1959. Stan was trained as an electronics technician who specialized in radio communications. He worked in the advanced consumer electronics sales field for over forty years. Stan has lived in Greensburg, Pennsylvania all of his life.

In the late 1960s, he acted as the telephone UFO sighting report investigations coordinator for the UFO Research Institute of Pittsburgh. Stan began in the field investigations of UFOs and other mysterious events in 1965, and is the primary investigator of the December 9, 1965 UFO crash-recovery incident that occurred near Kecksburg, Pennsylvania.

In 1969, Gordon established a UFO Hotline for the public to report UFO sightings to him to investigate. In 1970, Gordon founded the Westmoreland County UFO Study Group (WCUFOSG), the first of three volunteer research groups which he would establish to investigate UFO sightings and other strange occurrences reported in Pennsylvania.

Since November 1993, Stan continues to investigate and document strange incidents from across the keystone state as an independent researcher. Gordon is a former PA State Director for the

CREEPY CRYPTIDS

Mutual UFO Network (MUFON) and was its first recipient in 1987 of the MUFON Meritorious Achievement in a UFO Investigation Award. Gordon has been involved with the investigation of thousands of mysterious encounters from across Pennsylvania. He was listed in the 2005 FATE Magazine special, The 100 Most Influential People in UFOlogy Today.

Stan has appeared on numerous local, national, and international TV shows including the Syfy Channel (formerly the Sci-Fi Channel), Discovery Channel, History Channel, and Fox News Channel. He has been featured on many television shows, including Unsolved Mysteries, Sightings, Inside Edition, A Current Affair, and Creepy Canada.

Some of the other shows Stan appeared on were the Close Encounters series on the Science Channel, Monsters & Mysteries in America on the Destination America Channel, Monumental Mysteries on the Travel Channel, In Search of Aliens on H2, and UFO Conspiracies on the Science Channel.

Stan has also appeared in numerous documentary films concerning the UFO, Bigfoot and cryptid topics including, "Invasion on Chestnut Ridge" from the Smalltown Monsters production company. Gordon has been a guest on many national and international radio shows, including the popular radio show Coast to Coast.

Gordon is also the producer of the award-winning video documentary, Kecksburg: The Untold Story. Stan is also the author of the books, Really Mysterious Pennsylvania, Silent Invasion: The Pennsylvania UFO-Bigfoot Casebook, and Astonishing Encounters: Pennsylvania's Unknown Creatures.

Since the late 1960s, Gordon has been lecturing to the public and presenting illustrated lectures locally and nationally to social and professional groups, schools, colleges, libraries, and conferences.

Stan Gordon

His lecture topics include a synopsis of the Kecksburg UFO crash-landing case, UFO and Bigfoot incidents, and mysterious creature encounters.

CREEPY CRYPTIDS

Stan Gordon

CONTACT INFORMATION

Stan is interested in receiving reports of UFOs, Bigfoot, Thunderbirds, black panthers, and any strange creature or mysterious encounter that has occurred in Pennsylvania. He can be reached through the following avenues:

Mailing Address: Stan Gordon, P.O. Box 936, Greensburg, PA 15601

Phone: 724-838-7768

E-mail:
paufo@comcast.net
sightings@stangordon.info

Website: www.stangordon.info

Books and DVDs

Stan Gordon's books and DVD are available through www.amazon.com or www.barnes&noble.com. Personalized and/or autographed copies can be obtained at www.stangordon.info

CREEPY CRYPTIDS

Stan Gordon

INDEX

Allegheny County	115, 118, 146–147
Allegheny National Forest	154
Allegheny River	38
Apollo	197
Armstrong	42, 103–104, 132–133, 162, 164
Beaverdale	88
Belle Vernon	122–123
Big Run	120
Blair County	16
Blairsville	134, 176–177
Bloomsburg	72
Butler County	37, 118, 152, 170
Cambria County	40, 50, 60, 88, 141
Chestnut Ridge	1, 7–8, 36, 41, 48, 54–55, 59, 70, 76, 83, 91–92, 106, 108, 112, 121–122, 143, 165, 175, 177–183, 197, 204
Cook Forest	173
Cranberry	37
Delmont	57, 111, 136
Derry	8, 41, 69, 80, 106–108, 112, 119, 122, 142, 165, 175, 177, 181
Derry Ridge	41
Donegal	172
Dunbar	177
East Brady	38, 118
Ebensburg	50
Fairchance	36, 85, 92, 177
Fayette City	76
Fayette County	7, 36, 42, 51, 59, 76, 78, 83, 91–92, 103, 127–129, 134, 138, 177–178
Forest County	71
Greene County	49, 130
Greensburg	1, 9, 13, 18, 22, 27, 31, 80, 114, 119, 136, 148, 188, 192, 197, 203, 207
Hempfield Township	24
Herminie	15
Homer City	35, 177

CREEPY CRYPTIDS

Hopwood	51
Huntingdon County	126, 145
Indiana County	35–36, 87, 134, 136, 166, 169, 177, 181
Irwin	62, 65
Jeannette	23, 42, 119
Jefferson County	120, 173
Johnstown	40, 50, 60
Kinzua Lake	126
Kittanning	23
Lake Erie	126
Latrobe	29–30, 45, 54, 163, 177–178, 180
Laurel Highlands	140, 175, 178, 183, 186
Laurel Ridge	40, 178, 182–183
Ligonier	40, 57–58, 75–76, 121, 170, 177
Madison	34
Markleysburg	59
Masontown	73, 78
Mon Valley	108, 111, 123
Monessen	39, 123
Monongahela River	39, 43, 123, 126–128, 130
Mount Pleasant	21, 39, 57, 69
Mud Pike	85–86, 92, 94
Murrysville	61
Nanty Glo	61
Nemacolin	130
North Huntingdon	26, 30–31, 65, 95–96
Ohio Township	68
Ohiopyle	177
Parker	38
Pittsburgh	11–12, 35, 40, 42–43, 68, 81, 98–99, 102–103, 108, 111, 115, 118, 125–128, 140, 146–149, 166, 198, 203
Point Pleasant	118, 146, 151–152
Quebec Run Wilds	83, 85
Rankin Bridge	128, 130
Raystown Lake	126
Rockton Mountain	81–82
Sewickley Township	119
South Fork	60
Springdale	41
Spruce Creek	145

Sutersville	44, 49
Uniontown	42, 177
Warren County	126
Washington County	97
Waynesburg	25
West Newton	37, 90–91, 105
West Virginia	118, 146, 151, 177
Westmoreland County	11, 15, 22, 37, 45, 49, 54, 75, 80, 87, 91, 104–105, 108, 112, 119, 126, 136, 142, 159, 165, 175, 177, 179, 185, 203
White, PA	138, 140
Whitney	45
Worthington	164
York County	44
Youngstown	48, 54, 70, 177
Youngwood	171

www.ingramcontent.com/pod-product-compliance
Lightning Source LLC
Chambersburg PA
CBHW071915290426
44110CB00013B/1369